A Guide to "The Office": Season Three

By Kristina Benson

A Guide to "The Office": Season Three

ISBN: 978-1-60332-041-2

Edited By: Brooke Winger

Copyright© 2008 Equity Press. No part of this publication may be reproduced, stored in a retrieval system, or transmitted in any form or by any means (electronic, mechanical, photocopying, recording or otherwise) without either the prior written permission of the publisher or a license permitting restricted copying in the United States or abroad.

The scanning, uploading and distribution of this book via the internet or via any other means without the permission of the publisher is illegal and punishable by law. Please purchase only authorized electronic editions, and do not participate in or encourage piracy of copyrighted materials.

Trademarks: All trademarks are the property of their respective owners. Equity Press is not associated with any product or vender mentioned in this book.

Printed in the United States of America

Table of Contents

Gay Witch Hunt 6
    Synopsis 6
    Trivia 10
    Memorable Quotes 13

The Convention 16
    Synopsis 16
    Trivia 21
    Memorable Quotes 21

The Coup 25
    Synopsis 25
    Trivia 30

Grief Counseling 32
    Synopsis 32
    Trivia 36
    Memorable Quotes 37

Initiation 40
    Synopsis 40
    Trivia 45
    Memorable Quotes 47

Diwali 49
    Synopsis 49
    Trivia 51
    Memorable Quotes 52

Branch Closing 62
    Synopsis 62
    Producer's Cuts 66
    Trivia 68
    Memorable Quotes 69

The Merger 71
    Synopsis. 71
    Trivia 76
    Memorable Quotes 78

The Convict 80
    Synopsis 80
    Trivia 84
    Memorable Quotes 84

A Benihana Christmas 87
    Synopsis 87
    Trivia 92
    Memorable Quotes 94

Back from Vacation 98
    Synopsis 98
    Trivia 100
    Memorable Quotes 101

Traveling Salesman 106
    Synopsis 106
    Trivia 110
    Memorable Quotes 111

The Return 114
    Synopsis 114
    Trivia 117

Ben Franklin 122
    Synopsis 122
    Trivia 125
    Memorable Quotes 126

Phyllis' Wedding 129
    Synopsis 129
    Memorable Quotes 132

Business School 134
    Synopsis 134
    Trivia 137
    Memorable Quotes 138

Cocktails 140
    Synopsis 140
    Trivia 142

The Negotiation 143
    Synopsis 143
    Trivia 144

Safety Training 145
    Synopsis 145
    Deleted Scenes 146
    Memorable Quotes 147

Product Recall 150
    Synopsis 150
    Trivia 151
    Memorable Quotes 152

Women's Appreciation 155
    Synopsis 155
    Trivia 157
    Memorable Quotes 158

Beach Games 160
    Synopsis 160
    Trivia 162
    Memorable Quotes 162

The Job 165
    Synopsis 165
    Trivia 167
    Memorable Quotes 167

Index 170

Gay Witch Hunt

Gay Witch Hunt is the first episode of the third season of "The Office" (U.S. version). It is written by Greg Daniels and directed by Ken Kwapis. It first aired on September 21, 2006.

Synopsis

No longer a temp, Ryan Howard accepts the sales position that was left empty when Jim transferred to Stamford, Connecticut. Jim's absence is explained by a flashback in he and Pam kiss after the casino night. After informing Jim that she is still getting married, they say their goodbyes. In an interview, Dwight feigns tears over Jim's transfer, before indicating he's glad to be rid of him.

Michael calls Oscar Martinez "faggy" for preferring "Shakespeare in Love" to "Die Hard". Michael is asked by Toby not to use such terms, but insists it is a harmless synonym for "lame". Toby informs Michael that Oscar is homosexual and probably, as such, finds the word offensive.

Michael approaches Oscar at the copy machine and loudly apologizes for his comment, inviting Oscar to join him for a beer sometime. In a succession of short on-camera interviews, Oscar reveals that he is gay, Angela Martin indicates she hates the whole idea of homosexuality and the jowls of Kevin's face jiggle as he is unable to manage anything but "Oscar...is gay" through his giggles.

Meanwhile in Stamford, Jim's transfer came with a promotion and a modern office where his desk includes a window view. Co-worker Andy, who sits at a desk in front of Jim, calls him "Big Tuna", in reference to his lunch on is first day, a switch from his daily ham sandwich in Scranton. Co-worker Karen, who sits in the desk behind Jim, comments on the faces Jim makes on camera, which offers a demonstration that he's not fitting in to the new office in her opinion. Andy, meanwhile, discusses how he doesn't feel threatened by Jim as he thinks he's an ambitious know-it-all, and brags about his wild college days at Cornell.

Back in Scranton, Roy brings Pam her lunch in a short, awkward exchange. In an interview Pam explains that she got cold feet, called off the wedding, ended the relationship, and moved into her own apartment. As a result, Roy and Pam plan to eat for lunch the frozen wedding reception meals for the next five weeks.

A disheveled Roy is seen in a mug shot as he recalls how being dumped led him into a downward spiral of weight gain, beard growth and a DUI arrest. Roy claims he has recovered, laments that he didn't treat Pam right, and swears that he will win her back. Stanley's only comment on the break-up is that he gave the couple a toaster, was unable to return the discontinued model, and now has two toasters.

Dwight and Michael worry about homosexuals working in "The Office" without their knowledge. Dwight recalls Jim mentioning "gaydar" being available for purchase online, though Dwight is skeptical because past experience has told him that Jim doesn't always embrace the truth. They decide to telephone him in Stamford where Jim pretends to check the availability and reports that gaydar is sold out on the Internet. Also in Stamford, Jim recycles a joke he pulled on Dwight by encasing Andy's calculator in Jell-O. Andy gets violently upset and kicks a wastebasket as Jim silently returns to work, shaken up by Andy's reaction.

Kelly comes up to Oscar and informs him that he is "super-cool" for being gay. Jan Levinson gets irked at Michael, saying that he has outed Oscar, which should have been a personal decision of Oscar's. Toby points out that Oscar feels discriminated against by Angela. Employees gather around as Dwight looks at gay pornography per Michael's suggestion. Angela makes a homophobic comment which offends Oscar who bumps her as he walks past, sending Dwight into a brief frenzy.

Michael calls an emergency meeting in the conference room and informs the assembled they are all "homos". Pam looks to Ryan as she holds back shocked laughter, as she would have done with Jim, and is disappointed when he does not do the same. Michael tells Oscar to come out to "The Office" formally, "right here, however you want". Oscar does so, and says it is a part of his life he was not planning on sharing that day. Dwight, in turn requests that: "All the other office gays out themselves or I will do it for them."

Dwight then implies that Phyllis might be gay. Phyllis haughtily announces to all present that she is engaged to Bob Vance of Vance Refrigeration. Several employees congratulate her and a surprised, jealous Michael says there is hope for everyone. Following soon after, Phyllis explains to her former classmate, Michael, that many people thought he was gay in high school. Michael immediately springs to his defense after Phyllis describes the clothes he used to wear. Creed, in an interview, states that he probably made love to a man during the 1960s, as he made love to many women outdoors, in the mud and rain.

Oscar decides he can no longer work at the branch and announces such, but as he begins to leave, Michael stops him and tries to hug as a show of acceptance. Oscar blows up and calls Michael "small" which silences the staff in discomfort and reduces Michael to tears. Oscar apologizes and reciprocates the hug. In an interview tidbit, Dwight hypothesizes on whether or not Michael too is gay. Believing the hug insufficient, Michael tells the staff to "watch this, and burn this into your brains", and kisses a struggling, reluctant Oscar on the mouth. Dwight, who was apparently moved by Michael's actions, consequently attempts to kiss Oscar. In interviews, Dwight believes Michael is his first gay friend. Michael says any two people who want to be together should be together. He concludes by saying, "That's what she said...or he said."

Pam looks longingly at Ryan's desk, as Jim simultaneously glances at an empty seat next to him during a humorless diversity training conducted by Mr. Brown in Stamford. Glancing through his office blinds, Michael sees Oscar catch a ride from Gil, and muses, "Oscar's roommate...I wonder if he knows?" Oscar reveals in an interview that Jan gave him three months paid vacation and use of a company car in exchange for signing an agreement not to sue the company about his forced outing. In Oscar's words, "it pays to be gay".

In the final minutes of the show, Dwight opens a package from Jim, a novelty "gaydar" machine fashioned from a metal detector and lettered with the prefixes "Homo" and "Hetero". He confirms the device on Oscar, but is dumbfounded when the device goes off as he inadvertently swipes it across his own crotch. Pam notices and smiles.

Trivia

The shooting draft script of this episode was 33 pages, according to the TV Guide.

The cast and crew worked hard to keep the new season's plot elements from leaking and didn't even show clips of the episode until a few days before the premiere. However, in a New York Times article about producer Ben Silverman on September 17, it was written that, in the new season, Jim "was going to be in a long-distance relationship" with Pam, which pretty much revealed that Jim took the Stamford position.

The flashback footage of the aftermath of Jim and Pam's kiss in last season's "Casino Night" episode is actually new footage shot a few months after the episode aired. The main giveaways are that the kiss is different and Jim's hair is slightly shorter than in the original episode. Also, the lighting and camera positioning is different.

The kiss between Michael and Oscar was improvised. Jenna Fischer explained in her MySpace blog: "Steve (Carell) just went into that bit on the fly. It was brilliant! Those looks of shock/giddiness/confusion on our faces are REAL. We were all on the edge of our seats wondering what would happen next. I can't believe we held it together for as long as we did. I'm not sure we've ever laughed so hard on set."

On Angela's MySpace blog, she spoke of Oscar's three months absence: "Yes. On the show he and his partner, Gil, are going on a three-month trip to Europe. In real life, Oscar Nunez sold a TV show to Comedy Central. I believed it's called "Halfway House". It is an improv comedy. And he stars in it. They are shooting it right now but he will be back to ol' Dunder Mifflin at some point."

This episode marks the second time an expletive has been censored, the first time was in "Diversity Day" and the censored word was "boner". It would happen again in "A Benihana Christmas".

In the season two episode "Dwight's Speech", Ryan notes that Jim eats the same ham and cheese sandwich every day. In this episode, we see that Jim has adventurously tried a tuna sandwich only to be given a permanent nickname "Big Tuna" because of it. Jim also notes he's been promoted at Stamford, though in "Health Care", he noted that moving up in the company would make paper sales his career, a move which would cause him to "jump in front of a train."

In his interview, Andy reminisces about when he was attending Cornell University and singing in an cappella group named "Here Comes Treble". Although no such group exists or has ever existed at Cornell, there is an all-girl group called "Nothing But Treble".

Dwight says he was unable to tell that Oscar is gay because he was "not dressed in women's clothes." However, in "Halloween" Oscar wears a dress and a woman's wig as his costume.

Michael mentions him watching the gay-oriented TV series "The L Word" and "Queer As Folk" as proof that he has an open attitude toward homosexuals.

During a meeting in the Stamford office, the unnamed older woman seated to Jim's right has a hair-do and outfit similar to Pam's usual style.

Near the end of the episode, the character Mr. Brown has his second (but brief) appearance in the series, the first being in the

"Diversity Day" episode from season one. He is going over the meaning of "HERO", which was part of his diversity training course. Also, Jim looks towards an empty seat next to him and then his shoulder and smiles. This is also in reference to "Diversity Day" when Pam unintentionally fell asleep with her head on Jim's shoulder.

Memorable Quotes

Michael Scott: I call everybody faggy. Why would anyone find that offensive?
Toby: I think Oscar would like it if you just used "lame" or something.
Michael Scott: But that's what faggy means!

Michael Scott: You don't call retarded people retards. It's bad taste. You call your friends retards when they are acting retarded. And I consider Oscar a friend.

Michael Scott: Did you know that gay used to mean happy? When I was growing up it meant "lame". And now it means a man who makes love to other men. We're all homos. Homo sapiens.

Dwight Schrute: Jim told me you can buy gaydar online.
Michael Scott: That's ridiculous.
Dwight Schrute: Probably. He didn't tell the truth a lot.
Michael Scott: Let's call him and get the website.
Dwight Schrute: Definitely.

A Guide to "The Office": Season Three

Ryan Howard: Yeah, I'm not a temp anymore. I got Jim's old job. Which means at my ten year high school reunion, it will not say "Ryan Howard is a temp". It will say "Ryan Howard is a junior sales associate and a midrange paper supply firm".

Creed: I'm not offended by homosexuality. In the 60's I made love to many, many women - often outdoors, in the mud and the rain...and it's possible a man slipped in. [shrugs] There'd be no way of knowing.

Michael Scott: The company has made it my responsibility today to put an end to 100,000 years of being weirded out by gays.

Jim Halpert: I can't say whether Dunder Mifflin paper is less flammable, sir, but, I can assure you that it's certainly not more flammable.

Michael Scott: I need to know who else is gay. I don't want to offend anyone else.
Dwight Schrute: You could assume everyone is, and not say anything offensive.
Michael Scott: Yeah. I'm sure everyone would appreciate me treating them like they were gay.

Phyllis: I'm getting married to Bob Vance of Vance Refrigeration.

Michael Scott: That's great! Congratulations. That is great and frankly... kinda amazing. See... everybody has a chance.

Michael Scott: Gay porn, straight porn, it's all goooood. I don't particularly get into this, but you know what, I totally see the merit. And actually, it is quite beautiful.

Stanley: I got them a toaster. They called off the wedding and gave the toaster back to me. I tried to return the toaster to the store, and they said they no longer sold that kind of toaster. So now my house has got two toasters.

Michael Scott: I watch the L Word...I watch Queer as [bleep].
Toby: That's not what it's called.

The Convention

The Convention is the second episode of the third season of "The Office" (U.S. version). Written by Gene Stupnitsky and Lee Eisenberg and directed by Ken Whittingham, it first aired September 28, 2006.

Synopsis

Michael happens to catch Angelina Jolie's appearance on "Oprah", and is inspired by her words to adopt a Chinese baby. After Pam convinces him to give the idea a little more thought, Michael implies that he and Pam should conceive a baby together if neither of them has a child in ten years. Pam rejects the suggestion, as well as his revision of the suggestion, which says that perhaps they should wait twenty years. She finally agrees to the scenario when Michael suggests thirty years.

Michael and Dwight receive per diem money from Angela for their train trip to Philadelphia for the Northeastern Mid-Market Office Supply Convention. Ryan reviews Michael's checklist of his luggage for the trip, including three boxes of condoms and his white "fun jeans" which are folded on a hanger and wrapped in plastic. Angela is angry with Dwight for leaving when they'd had plans.

Meanwhile, Kelly is looking forward to the double date she has arranged with herself, Ryan, Pam, and Kelly's neighbor, Alan, who is a cartoonist for the local newspaper. Kelly urges Pam not to sleep with Alan on the first date. Pam admits in an interview that she is nervous and has not been on a first date in nine years. Overhearing date chat, Michael suggests Pam wear her wedding dress as a joke, and Dwight chimes in that her veil should complete the ensemble. Pam steadfastly says she will wear the same clothes she wore to work that day, and Michael tells her to unbutton her top button to "let those things breathe a little." Noting that Jim will be at the convention, Michael asks Pam if she wants him to relay a message, then teases her as she is only able to get out an "Um..." before he interrupts her.

Creed sees Angela giving the per diem money to Michael and Dwight and wonders how he can get a piece of the action. After being informed that the cash is for the Philadelphia trip, he and Meredith bash the city of brotherly love. An indignant Angela storms out of the room, despite earlier mentioning a Martin family phrase — "The slow train from Philly" — used to indicate a potential prostitute in the vicinity. She leaves behind a plate of food that Creed immediately begins to eat. He informs Meredith that "Andrea is "The Office" bitch" and proceeds to introduce himself, apparently not recognizing Meredith from the many years they have worked together in the same small office.

In Philadelphia, Michael calls out "traitor" as a friendly greeting to Jim in the hotel lobby. Dwight asks him if he's made any sales and Jim says he has "sold about $40,000". Dwight doesn't believe him; however, he still claims that he has completed $40,000 in sales so far. Michael also chats briefly with Stamford regional manager Josh, who informs Michael that should his branch merge with the Scranton branch, he will find a position within his new Stamford branch for Michael. A cause for concern washes across Michael's face when he hears this. Michael also queries Jan about "the 800-pound gorilla in the room," Carol. Saying that Jan must keep her hands off of him during the convention, Jan tells Michael to move away from her, and Michael thanks her for her cooperation. Angela secretly arrives at the convention incognito under the name "Jane Doe".

Michael and Dwight meet Jerome Bettis, who is signing autographs at the convention. Bettis is reluctant to commit to attending Michael's party in Room 308. Michael informs Dwight that Bettis is nicknamed "The Bus" because of the pro-footballer's fear of flying that leads him to take busses even to games that are very far apart. During lunch, Michael updates Jim on the Scranton happenings including Ryan taking over Jim's position and desk. Jim sends his regards and Michael promises to relay them. Jim begins to ask how a former co-worker is doing, but briefly hesitates before the name, eventually choosing to ask about Toby. Michael responds by asking if Toby was why Jim left, or if he had considered bosses, leading to an inquiry as to what Jim thought of Josh compared to Michael. Jim states that it's not a competition.

Michael assigns Dwight to dig up dirt on Josh. Michael takes a work-related phone call from Pam, and Jim is surprised when Michael wishes her luck on her date. Dwight informs Michael his contact at the sheriff's office isn't volunteering this day.

Michael promotes a Scranton v. Stamford paper airplane game at the Hammermill booth, but his plane crashes shortly after takeoff. Jim and Josh head off to other business and Michael brings the Hammermill salesperson to his room where he shares his emotions over Jim leaving his branch and discusses paper with the rep. As a result, Michael surprises the entire Dunder Mifflin contingent with the news he broke Staples' exclusive hold on Hammermill products and secured a deal with the company, impressing even Jan. Michael even proceeds to tip the hotel waiter with his company per diem of $100 as just another way to try and impress Jan.

Jim has Dwight's room key and walks in on Angela, who is naked, and mistakes for a prostitute. Embarrassed, he immediately leaves the room. He is shocked by the experience and tries to think of someone to call to share the news.

Back in the Scranton office, Kevin expresses to Toby his lust for Pam now that she has started dating again. Toby responds by musing about asking her out and eventually deciding not to. Phyllis suggests Pam order an expensive entree at dinner to show she's worth it. Stanley concludes that an expensive dinner requires Pam to "put out." Phyllis agrees with this assessment.

While on the double date, Kelly appears to be the only one having a good time, chatting and shoving food into Ryan's mouth. Ryan, however, seems mortified. Pam is nervous and talks to her dull date who states that he gets his comic strip ideas from the world around him, or in a dream. On a napkin, he sketches a scene referencing the 2003 freedom fries controversy, and states that it works on many levels. He reveals people tell him not to be edgy in his cartoons, but it is the only way he knows. When Pam politely laughs, Alan appears to briefly look down her shirt, and in response, Pam buttons it higher. Meanwhile, at the convention, Jim arrives on the third floor to thumping electronic music and finds Michael sitting Indian-style playing with convention swag by strobe light. He says people have been wandering in and out of the party. Jim asks for a drink, and as Michael serves him a Cosmo, says he realizes that their boss-employee friendship was brief but not something Jim wanted to keep. Jim tells him he did not leave because he is a bad boss and calls Michael a great boss, and he left after he laid himself on the line to Pam and she rejected him, twice.

Michael says he will talk to Pam, which Jim asks him not to. Michael also suggests that Jim talk to Roy, because Roy knows exactly how he is feeling. Jim says he might. He and Michael make up and their renewed friendship is announced to party guests from the Hammermill staff.

Pam's date ends with Alan picking his teeth and telling her to bring her sketches next time. She informs the camera that she has not found a love connection.
A final scene finds Michael and Dwight preparing the black light for the Room 308 party. The light reveals stains covering the walls, comforter and headboard. Dwight speculates the stains are blood, urine, or semen, and a Michael says he hopes they are urine.

Trivia

This episode was shot immediately after the Emmys. Angela says in her Myspace blog that the In Style party looked like a really expensive wedding.

According to an article in "Entertainment Weekly", producers had considered using this episode to reveal that Angela was pregnant. Evidentially, they rejected the idea.

Jerome Bettis is actually nicknamed The Bus because he is good at getting touchdowns.

Memorable Quotes

Michael Scott: You know what Pam, if in ten years I haven't had a baby, and you haven't had a baby...
Pam Beasley: No, Michael.
Michael Scott: Twenty years?
Pam Beasley: No, Michael.
Michael Scott: Thirty.
Pam Beasley: Sure
Michael Scott: It's a deal.

Michael Scott: Guess where I am going? I will give you a hint. It is a booze-fueled sex romp where anything goes. You are correct sir! I'm headed to Philadelphia for the annual

Northeastern mid-market office supply convention. And Jim Halpert is going to be coming which will be fun, poor little guy... he's been stuck working under Josh, the poor man's Michael Scott, as he is known around my condo.

Michael Scott [talking about Jim]: I was shocked when he told me he was transferring to Stamford. It's like with fireman, you don't leave your brothers behind. Even if you find out that there is a better fire in Connecticut.

Jim Halpert: You know, when I saw Dwight I realized how stupid and petty all those pranks I pulled on him were. And then he spoke. I wonder how hard it would be to get a copy of his room key.

Kevin Malone: So did you hear?
Toby Flenderson: What?
Kevin Malone: Pam's back on the market again.
Toby Flenderson: Really, she's dating.
Kevin Malone: If I wasn't engaged I would so hit that.

Jim Halpert: Wow!
Michael Scott: Hey Hey!
Jim Halpert: That is a lot of liquor.
Michael Scott: Yeah!
Jim Halpert: And a dart board.
Michael Scott: Well that's how we do it in Scranton, or did you forget? [rapping] Ain't no party like a Scranton party, 'cuz a Scranton party don't stop. Huh huh huh!

Michael Scott: I love inside jokes. I'd like to be a part of one some day.

Michael Scott: SWAG! Stuff - we - all - get. I basically decorated my condo for free with all of my SWAGGGG! Check it out.

Jan: Well Michael, I...underestimated you.
Michael: Well maybe next time you'll estimate me.

Michael Scott: Some people need dozens of friends to say "Hey, look at me I'm popular." But not me, I'm very picky, I need 3, maybe 2. When you meet that someone special you'll just know because a real relationship can't be forced. It should just come about effort-et-lessly.

Michael Scott: Wow, what are all those stains?
Dwight Schrute: Blood, urine or semen.
Michael Scott: Oh, God. I hope it's urine.

Angela: In the Martin family, we like to say, "Looks like someone took the slow train from Philly." That's code for "check out the slut." [swats at a fly] Why are there flies in here?

Creed: [referring to Angela, while speaking to longtime co-worker Meredith] Andrea is "The Office" bitch. You'll get used to her. [extends hand] Creed.

Jim Halpert: Oh my god! Dwight got a hooker! Oh my god, I gotta call... I gotta call somebody. I don't know who to call... Dwight got a HOOKER!

Phyllis: [talking to Pam about her upcoming date] You should order the most expensive thing on the menu, so he knows you're worth it.
Stanley: If you do that, you're gonna have to put out.
Phyllis: [pause] Oh yeah, you'll have to put out.

Dwight Schrute: (referring to Jerome Bettis) Why do they call him "The Bus"?
Michael Scott: Because he's afraid to fly.

The Coup

The Coup is the third episode of the third season of "The Office" (U.S. version). It aired on October 5, 2006.

Synopsis

Pam prepares microwave popcorn as Michael comments on his dire hunger. He pulls a DVD copy of "Varsity Blues" from his office safe, and calls it the only cure for Monday blues. Pam explains in an interview that Michael began Movie Monday with training videos, and continued the tradition with an ill-received medical video, six repeats of a single episode of Entourage and finally a feature film in thirty-minute increments. Prior to the screening, Michael selects Kevin to summarize the previous plot points in the movie in order to bring the audience up to speed.

Angela states her opposition to Movie Monday, and indeed is the only employee not in attendance when Jan pops in to the branch unexpectedly. Jan scolds Michael despite his explanation that productivity increases following the screenings as employees must work harder due to the lost time.

In interviews, Angela and Dwight both note that Jan seems to have a vendetta against Michael for his choosing Carol over her, and fear it might affect the Scranton branch. Angela summons Dwight to the break room, where they speak as usual with their backs turned. Angela tells Dwight she fears for their jobs under

Michael's leadership, and tells Dwight to speak to Jan about taking over the branch. In the parking lot, Dwight calls Jan on her cell phone when she is an hour out of Scranton. She does not want to talk, but listens when he says it concerns Michael. Dwight instructs her to shop at the nearby Liz Claiborne outlet store — which he has deduced to be a favorite brand of hers — until he can reach her. He then Michael he is visiting a new dentist who works far away, so he will be gone for about three hours.

Jan and Dwight sit at a nearby diner where he orders two plates of waffles and begins to propose taking over the branch. Pouring syrup maniacally and proceeding to eat in a deliberate way for effect, he states that he could do the job better by firing half the staff, to whom he swears no loyalty since he doesn't care about any of his co-workers. As the meeting ends and Dwight sloppily devours his meal in front of her, he urges Jan to check out a new Ann Taylor outlet store nearby, as he has noticed she is fond of the brand's earrings. Jan calls Michael, relays to him the details of the entire meeting and demands he get his branch under control.

Meanwhile, the Stamford branch has its own distraction, the computer war game "Call of Duty", being played under the guise of a team-building exercise. New to the game, Jim's playing is poor and he mentions video games weren't played at his former office. He does, however, reveal a prank in which he and Pam hummed the same high note in the hopes of prompting Dwight to have his hearing checked, an endeavor Pam dubbed "pretendinitis".

Back in Scranton, Pam shops online for new clothes at Kelly's suggestion. Upon the clothes' arrival, Kelly demands that Pam perform a lunchtime fashion show. Though Kelly, Phyllis and Meredith compliment her on her clothes, Pam says she may end up returning them. Roy enters the breakroom and tells Pam she looks pretty. Kelly asks if that is his third soda of the day, to which he doesn't respond.

In Stamford, Jim manages to kill a player in "Call of Duty", but the thrill is short-lived as he is told he's killed a fellow teammate on the German side. As another game starts up, Josh calls Jim and Andy for an impromptu huddle about game strategy. Andy blames defeat on "the new guy," and as Jim reveals his use of a sniper rifle, both co-workers react in disgust, with Josh scolding Jim for using the weapon on an inappropriate map, and Andy claiming he is going to shoot Jim "for real."

Upon Dwight's return, a calm but clearly offended Michael initially tries to make him admit he didn't go to the dentist by doling out M&M's and asking for the dentist's name, to which Dwight replies "Crentist." When Michael notes how the name sounds strangely like "dentist," Dwight reasons it may have been why he chose the profession.

Later, Michael tells Dwight that Jan has called to demote him to Dwight's position as Assistant (to the) Regional Manager, and

Dwight should be expecting a call from Corporate to take over as acting Regional Manager. Announcing it to "The Office", multiple people question Dwight's selection, and even Kevin expresses concern that Michael possibly losing his condo. Angela is the only one to congratulate Dwight, though later, when she says in private that they could make a difference together, he corrects her to say he will make a difference. Though Angela seems upset at first, she then seems pleased as Dwight offers her to be in charge of the female staff.

Michael eventually reveals the hoax when Dwight casually refuses the keys to Michael's Corporate Chrysler Sebring convertible, and insults the vehicle due to its poor gas mileage and impracticality in Scranton's climate. Taking the remark personally, Michael blows up at Dwight after he refuses to take back what he said, especially after Dwight previously stated that he loved the car (a sycophantic lie meant to appease Michael). In turn, Dwight begins to beg for his job and grovels at the floor for Michael's forgiveness, offering to do his laundry for a month, then a year, to which Michael responds he has a laundry machine. Michael forces him to "Hug it out, bitch," which, Michael tells the camera, is what men say and do to each other after a fight (this is a reference to Michael's obsession with "Entourage"). Dwight returns quickly to being Michael's loyal right-hand man at the next Movie Monday, as Angela notices in disappointment.

Pam decides to return to dressing her usual way at work when Creed walks over to her desk, blatantly looks down her shirt and refuses to leave. Pam covers up with a sweater and decides to keep her new clothes for wearing only when she is outside of "The Office".

Jim still can't get the basics of the game, and Karen catches him jumping in a corner trying to shoot with a smoke grenade. Karen tells the camera to "look at how cute he is," before telling Jim to turn his character around. Requesting any last words, she shoots his character point blank, causing "You killed Jim Halpert" to appear on her screen. Jim then turns to the camera and whispers "psychopath." At the end of the day, Jim pretends to throw a grenade towards her desk when leaving, to which she tosses a few paper clips in the resulting explosion. They laugh, and after he leaves, she still gives a slight wave and continues to stare at the exit.

Deciding he still harbored resentment towards Dwight, Michael forces him to solemnly stand atop a box with a "LIAR" sign dangling from his neck, in addition to one year of indentured servitude as a launderer.

A Guide to "The Office": Season Three

Trivia

Andy's Call of Duty screen name is "Here Comes Treble" after his a capella group mentioned in the season premiere.

Karen's screen name is "KarentheJimSlayer"

This appears to be the first (and only) episode of "The Office" known to be set on a Monday.

Michael makes "The Office" watch a single episode of Entourage six times.

In a deleted scene on NBC.com, Jim kills Karen's apparently idle character, and then sees that Karen is talking to Jan. Jan then presses the button that kills Jim's character.

Jim seems to have never heard of "Call of Duty", though a copy of the Mac-compatible version of "Call of Duty: United Offensive" is clearly visible on the desk in Jim's room in the season two episode "E-mail Surveillance".

Angela Kinsey did an interview that ended up being deleted from the final cut of the episode. In it, she talks about this "friend" of hers that introduced her to this show, "Star Trek". "Well, there is this guy named Spock and he is very honorable and brave," Kinsey paraphrases, "And he stands up for what he thinks is right. And she just wishes that "someone" in "The Office" could be more like Spock." Kinsey continues, "I thought it was a cute glimpse into Dwight and Angela's courtship. I can see her being very resistant to Sci-fi but she watches these Star Trek episodes because they are important to Dwight."

A Guide to "The Office": Season Three

Grief Counseling

Grief Counseling is the fourth episode of the third season of "The Office" (U.S. version). It aired on October 12, 2006.

Synopsis

Michael pretends to be walking down the stairs behind a stack of paper boxes under the guise of retrieving a pencil "from the warehouse" for Ryan. An overzealous Dwight prompts a second go-around of the joke, and Pam keeps the joke alive, pleading for a cup of coffee, which Michael crawls to the break room to retrieve. In an interview, he likens himself to Bette Midler in "For the Boys": "Gotta keep the troops entertained." Upon his return crawl, Pam requests cream and sugar in her coffee.

Michael flips through his Rolodex and starts to flirt with Jan on the phone after she tells him "We've lost Ed Truck." At first he thinks that Jan has lost his contact information, but soon it becomes clear that the former Scranton branch manager has passed away. Kelly and Phyllis console Michael after he breaks the news to a mostly unmoved staff. He announces he'll be in his office for consolation pop-ins, but with no takers he wanders to the reception desk and engulfs Pam in an awkward too-long hug, telling her Truck was "almost 70, so ... circle of life."

Meanwhile, at a staff meeting in Stamford, Karen irritates Josh when she neglects to compile a supply list for Fairfield County

Schools. She is irritated when Josh asks Jim to make sure that she completes the task. Jim agrees and Andy calls him a suck-up in a thinly disguised cough (*cough* "suck-up" *cough* etc). In the Stamford break room, Karen is disappointed to discover that the vending machine is out of salt and vinegar potato chips, and turns her ire on Jim, telling him that her snack food needs do not fall under his authority. He counters that he does have that power, and no work shall be completed until the chips she requires are procured.

At the Scranton office, Michael makes a comment on Creed's age, but the mood changes when Creed mentions Truck was decapitated after flying down Route 6 after a few too many, sliding his vehicle beneath an 18-wheeler. Dwight steals Michael's thunder with a blunt announcement of the latest news. In an interview, Dwight says that he would like to be frozen, even in pieces, if he died, so that he may one day be reanimated with the knowledge to avoid the same death in the future.

On speakerphone with Jan, Michael laments the fact that the staff receives a whole day off in honor of Martin Luther King, Jr., "and he didn't even work here." On his desk is a decade-old Dunder-Mifflin newsletter with a full-color photo of Truck and a mulleted Michael above a headline reading "Michael Scott achieves top sales honors for third straight quarter."

Michael suggests a full-size statue of Truck with illuminated eyes and mobile arms be erected to honor the late former branch manager. Jan finds the idea unrealistic and hangs up, but an ever-resourceful Dwight prepares a schematic of a 2/3 size Truck robot with a six-foot extension cord in case it were to turn against the staff.

Back in Stamford, Jim phones potential chip sources as Karen prepares to give up the search. Gentle taunting lures her back in as she assures him "I am not a quitter."

Michael disgusts some employees by imagining the bloodbath Truck endured when his "cappa was de-tated ... from his head." He summons the staff to a makeshift grief counseling session involving a collapsible Hoberman Sphere ball. Expounding on his feeling at the loss of his beloved ex-boss, he says it "feels like my heart has been dropped into a bucket of boiling tears and someone else is hitting my soul in the crotch with a frozen sledgehammer and a third guy is punching me in the griefbone, but no one hears me because I'm terribly, terribly alone."

Roy pulls Pam away from the session under the guise of a radiator issue in her new hatchback. In the parking lot, Pam and Roy have a chat about her car's airbags and he asks if she's "still driving too fast." Upon her return to the grief session, she finds Michael has put the whole ceremony on hold because "we wait for a family member." Stanley refuses to play Michael's grief game but Dwight gladly tells the group he absorbed another fetus while still in the womb, making him as strong as a man combined with a baby. Pam expounds on the death of her aunt and Ryan tells the tale of his cousin Mufasa who was trampled by wildebeests, horrifying those "in the audience ... of what happened." His story echoes "The Lion King", and he says it would take over an hour and a half to tell the whole story. Eager to play along, Kevin poorly disguises "Weekend at Bernie's" as his tale of grief, angering Michael.

Toby informs Michael that death is a part of life, and uses an example of a bird that flew into a Dunder-Mifflin first-floor window that morning. Mortified that Toby did not investigate the bird's health, Michael charges outside, picks up the deceased animal and attempts to resuscitate it via mouth-to-mouth, rebuking Dwight's pleas to drop the germ-ridden corpse.

When attempts to revive the bird fail, Michael schedules a 4 p.m. parking lot funeral for the bird, despite staff complaints that they all still have a lot of work to complete. Dwight breaks off the bird's beak in an attempt to stuff it through the pop-tab of an empty soda can. In an interview he comments on the resourcefulness of farm-dwellers such as himself and reveals his grandfather was reburied in an oil drum.

Pam fashions a makeshift coffin and reads a prepared speech that comforts Michael. She mentions that although the bird was an unknown among the staff, it surely did not die alone as it had the company of other birds, and likely wanted to get into Dunder-Mifflin Scranton in order to serenade the staff with a song. Michael is noticeably moved by the speech and his eyes well with tears. Dwight interrupts her to state that the deceased was "not a songbird." Pam accompanies Dwight who plays "On the Wings of Love" on his recorder. The coffin is placed in a box of shredded paper and set afire.

Karen finds a bag of salt and vinegar potato chips on her desk and, in a voiceover, Jim says he traced the chips from the manufacturer to the distributor to the vending machine company to an adjacent office building.

Dwight extinguishes the funeral pyre and coffin before ordering warehouse employees to "get a broom, mush."

Trivia

When Karen is at the vending machine, a bag of the chips she desired — Herr's Salt and Vinegar — can be seen along the left hand side of the vending machine.

Although Dwight claims that the bird given the funeral is "not a songbird", it appears to be a sparrow, which actually is a songbird.

It is revealed that Michael, Phyllis, and Creed have worked in "The Office" the longest.

Jokingly in his family member death story, Kevin says the plot of "Weekend at Bernie's". In a deleted scene for "The Fire", he states that it is one of his top five favorite movies (along with "Weekend at Bernie's II").

Memorable Quotes

Michael Scott: I lost Ed Truck... and it feels like somebody took my heart and dropped it into a bucket of boiling tears... and at the same time, somebody else is hitting my soul in the crotch with a frozen sledgehammer... and then a third guy walks in and starts punching me in the grief bone... and I'm crying, and nobody can hear me, because I'm terribly, terribly...terribly alone.

Dwight Schrute: When I die, I want to be frozen. And if they have to freeze me in pieces, so be it. I will wake up stronger than ever, because I will have used that time, to figure out exactly why I died. And what moves I could have used to defend myself better now that I know what hold he had me in.

Michael Scott: I don't understand. We have a day honoring Martin Luther King, but he didn't even work here.

Michael Scott: He leaves work, he's on his way home. WHAM, his cappa is detated from his head. **Dwight Schrute**: (to Angela) If my head ever comes off, I would like you to put it on ice.

Creed: It's a real shame about Ed huh.
Michael Scott: Yeah. It must really have you thinkin.
Creed: About what?

Michael Scott: The older you get, the bigger the chances you're gonna die. You knew that.
Creed: Ed was decapitated.
Michael Scott: What?
Dwight Schrute: Really?
Creed: He was drunk as a skunk, he was flying down Route 6. He slides under an 18 wheeler. Pop. Snaps right off.
Michael Scott: Oh my God.
Dwight Schrute: That is the way to go. Instant death. Very Smart.
Creed: You know a human can go on living for several hours after being decapitated.
Dwight Schrute: You're thinking of a chicken.

Creed: What did I say? Dwight Schrute: And how big do you want this robot?
Michael Scott: Lifesize.
Dwight Schrute: Mmm no. Better make it two-thirds. Easier to stop if it turns on us.
Dwight Schrute: Look. I gave him a 6 foot extension chord so he can't chase us.
Michael Scott: That's perfect.

Michael Scott: If I can get them depressed, then I'll have done my job.
Dwight Schrute: When my mother was pregnant with me, they did an ultrasound and found she was having twins. When they did another ultrasound a few weeks later, they discovered, that I had resorbed the other fetus. Do I regret this? No, I believe his

tissue has made me stronger. I now have the strength of a grown man and a little baby. Pam: If you wanna do something for the funeral...

Dwight Schrute: Yes, please.

Pam: Maybe you could play a song on your recorder.

Dwight Schrute: Excellent.

Pam: Do you have it with you?

Dwight Schrute: Always.

Michael Scott: Society teaches us that, having feelings and crying is bad and wrong. Well, that's baloney, because grief isn't wrong. There's such a thing as good grief. Just ask Charlie Brown.

Dwight Schrute: I'm sorry! I grew up on a farm! We killed a pig whenever we wanted bacon! And when my grandfather died, we buried him in an old oil drum! (pause) He would have fit if Michael had just given me another minute.

Initiation

Initiation is the fifth episode of the third season of "The Office" (U.S. version). It aired on October 19, 2006.

Synopsis

Dwight begins to quiz Ryan with brain teasers, but becomes frustrated and screams "Damnit!" when Ryan recites answers to the puzzles, many before the full question is asked.

Jan needles Michael about his productivity and presses him to enumerate his accomplishments during the previous workday. Michael says he "worked, went home to his condo, and Carol came over, and we had sex." Jan instructs Pam to log Michael's hourly activity "so we can analyze it at Corporate". Jan walks out of "The Office" as Pam begins to protest.

Dwight pesters Ryan about his excitement level for his first-ever sales call and informs the camera why he is so excited: Ryan has yet to make an ally within "The Office", and Dwight hopes to steer him clear of being a "slacker-loser-wiseass like Jim" and draft him in the "Dwight army of champions." That afternoon, Dwight drives Ryan to a beet field, smirks to the cameraman in the backseat and tells Ryan "Your journey begins now, sly fox."

At Dunder-Mifflin Stamford, Karen is annoyed when she realizes her chair squeaks and accuses Jim of a chair swap. He protests that he simply switched them back after she made the original switch. Karen promises to switch chairs while he's away from his desk, so he vows not to stand. He goes to the copy machine by rolling over on the chair.

On a phone call, Michael imitates Bill Cosby: "I love Jell-O puddin' pops. My son Theo loves puddin' pops, too." Pam shows the camera "Cosby Impression" for the 10:00 hour in the log.

Dwight forces Ryan to snatch a beet seed from his palm and plant it in a field. The Assistant (to the) Regional Manager tells the young salesman "just as you planted that seed, I shall plant my seed in you" to which the young salesman says "I don't think you know what you're saying." Dwight says the bad odor in the area is "called bull crap" and states that "clients can smell it from a mile away". Dwight suddenly announces he forgot something in his car and exuberantly dashes to where it is parked, gets in and speeds away.

A loudspeaker announces that free soft pretzels will be given away in the lobby. Stanley and Michael immediately head for the door. In interviews, Stanley proclaims that pretzel day is his favorite day of the year, Pam admits it is a big deal for some people and Michael says he cannot be productive when there is one thing in his brain which he just can't get out, especially when that one thing is soft pretzels.

A long pretzel line peeves Michael, and he and Stanley rebuff Phyllis' attempt to jump the line with Bob Vance of Vance

Refrigeration; Stanley momentarily overcomes his usual disdain for Michael and high-fives him. Pam asks Michael to use his time in line to authorize some checks, but he instead has her hold his place in line while he uses the restroom. She offers to brings him a pretzel if Michael returns to "The Office", but he explains that if she ordered his pretzel incorrectly "then ... this whole thing's blown." Shown to the camera, the productivity log now reads "Stood in Pretzel line" for the noon hour.

An angry Ryan walks alone up a dirt road, muttering to himself. He knocks on a barn door, and Dwight jumps out: "Congratulations, resourceful salesman! Welcome to Schrute Farm!" Having passed Dwight's second challenge, Ryan sits in a Victorian-era wheelchair and surmises that the apparition haunting the hallowed grounds is actually Dwight's cousin Mose. Dwight quizzes Ryan about Dunder-Mifflin, the death of company cofounder Robert Mifflin, the purpose of the DHARMA Initiative, and Michael's greatest fear, to which Ryan incorrectly answers "loneliness. Maybe women.""Wrong. The correct answer is nothing. I also would have accepted snakes," says Dwight. "You must vanquish fear."

Mose appears with the word "Fear" on his shirt in tape, and Dwight tells Ryan as his final test he must wrestle Mose to the ground. Ryan calls Dwight a freak and storms out, despite Dwight's protests and instructions to get inside a coffin. Mose remarks "he seemed nice," and Dwight asks "Where are all the animals?"

At Stamford, Karen begins to continually squeak her chair. Jim quickly begins to sing the chorus of The Cardigans' "Lovefool" (love me love me, say that you'll love me etc) despite Karen's objections that the song is unfair retaliation and "will be in her head all day." The camera pans to Andy, who is conducting and lip synching along with Jim's vocals, out of sight. In an interview, Andy completes the song's chorus — "I don't care 'bout anything but you" — and ponders the whereabouts of the band. Eventually the squeaky chair circulates over to Andy's desk when he isn't in the room.

Michael finally arrives at the front of the line and orders "The Works" — a pretzel with all 18 sweet toppings. Back upstairs, he plays energetic music, then suddenly emerges from his office and launches into a hyperactive, sugar-fueled speech filled with suggestions on improving office efficiency.

Inside his Trans Am, Dwight catches up with Ryan as he walks along the road, apologizes, and displays gifts Mose sent, including fresh eggs, fatback bacon, and "something he whittled," which appears to be a Venus figurine. After withstanding a significant amount of pleading, Ryan gets in the car where Dwight explains that the lack of a friendship with Jim was the main impetus for the initiation ceremony. Dwight then begins to give Ryan sales-call pointers which Ryan tries to memorize. His final advice is for Ryan to "K.I.S.S. — Keep It Simple Stupid."

Michael sleeps face-down on his desk, having succumbed to a post-pretzel carb crash. Jan phones for him, but Pam says he's on a sales call.

A dejected Ryan walks out of the sales call as Dwight tries to cheer him up. Ryan gripes that the potential client told him to his face that they didn't like him. In retaliation, Ryan begins to throw Mose's eggs at the building and CEO reserved parking sign. Surprised at Ryan's initiative, Dwight joins him, shouting "Oh no, no, no, Temp, you didn't," until two security guards saunter out, at which point the pair peel out of the parking lot in Dwight's Firebird. They go to a bar and drink boilermakers, and as a result of the day's events, Dwight no longer calls Ryan "Temp" but instead uses his given name.

At the end of the work day, Pam learns that Michael's antics helped him make a large sale. Having forgotten Kevin's phone extension, Jim calls Dunder-Mifflin's main number, hoping to leave him a voicemail regarding a fantasy football issue. Pam answers and says she's staying late because of her new assignment to chronicle Michael's work day, a copy of which she promises to send to Jim. The pair enjoys a long chat about her tiny apartment and her scary solo movie night in which she rented "28 Days Later" rather than "28 Days". They start to reconnect, but Ryan and Dwight, both exhausted, return to "The Office" for a few seconds and she loudly says goodbye to the pair as they exit. Jim misconstrues the exclamation, thinking it was meant for him, and they hang up.

Stanley then remarks in an interview that in 364 days, it will once again be Pretzel Day.

Trivia

Here are the brain teasers that Dwight asked Ryan:

1. There are two coins totaling 15 cents; one of them is not a nickel. What are they?
Answer: a nickel and a dime.

2. A man and his son get into a car accident. When they are at the hospital, the old surgeon says: "There's no way I can operate on this boy. He's my son." How can this be if he and his father both died? This riddle is also told in the series finale of the original version of "The Office", and in an episode of the Cosby Show.
Answer: the surgeon was a woman. Women can be doctors now. And they can vote!

3. A man hangs himself, and the detective finds a puddle of water, but nothing he could have stood on. How did this man hang himself?
Answer: He stood on a block of ice.

4. A hunter leaves his base camp one morning and travels one mile due south. He then turns and travels one mile due east. At this point, he shoots a bear. Taking the direct route, he travels

one mile due north and is back at the base camp. What kind of bear did he shoot?

Answer: a Polar bear.

According to the announcement made over "The Office"'s public address system, the complimentary soft pretzels are provided "as a thank you to our loyal tenants." The announcement is made by Billy Merchant, identified in "The Injury" as the Scranton Business Park properties manager.

While "testing" Ryan, one of the questions that Dwight asks him is what the DHARMA Initiative, from "Lost", is.

While in the pretzel line, Kelly tells Michael the plot of "Lazy Sunday", which is parodied by Michael and Dwight in the episode "The Merger". They call their parody "Lazy Scranton."

According to Dwight's trivia answer, Dunder-Mifflin co-founder Robert Mifflin killed himself, not because of depression, but because "he hated himself."

Michael revealed to Creed in "The Carpet" that his greatest fear is becoming his former boss.

The figurine Mose whittled as a part of his gift basket is actually a rendition of the Venus of Willendorf.

Dwight repeatedly calls Ryan "Temp" even though Ryan was hired permanently prior to "Gay Witch Hunt".

When Pam tells Jim that she can type 90 words per minute, he replies by saying that not even Mavis Beacon, the logotype persona for the typing program Mavis Beacon Teaches Typing, could type that fast. Coincidently, Jenna Fischer worked several years as a receptionist and types at 85 words per minute. Before Pam's typing speed was established, Fischer imagined Pam as not being able to type that fast and intentionally slowed down.

Memorable Quotes

Dwight Schrute: What is Michael Scott's greatest fear?
Ryan Howard: Loneliness... maybe women.

Dwight Schrute: Just think, that temp agency could have sent you anywhere!
Ryan Howard: I think about that all the time.

Dwight Schrute: Michael always says "K-I-S-S. Keep it simple, stupid." Great advice. Hurts my feelings every time.

Dwight Schrute: Just as you have planted your seed into the ground, I will plant my seed into you.
Ryan Howard: I don't think you realize what you're saying.

Kelly: Dwight's a freak!
Angela: No, YOU'RE A FREAK!

Stanley: I wake up every morning in a bed that's too small, drive my daughter to a school that's too expensive, and then I go to work to a job for which I get paid too little, but on pretzel day? Well, I like pretzel day.

Stanley: Only 364 days until my next pretzel.

Dwight Schrute: Why did Robert Mifflin commit suicide?!
Ryan Howard: He had depression.
Dwight Schrute: No! He hated himself! What... is the DHARMA Initiative?!

Dwight Schrute: Will Ryan become a loser, slacker like Jim or will he join the Dwight Army of Champions?

Michael Scott: [While eating a pretzel] It tastes so good in my mouth.
Stanley: That's what she said. [He and Michael laugh]

Diwali

Diwali is the sixth episode of the third season of "The Office" (U.S. version). It aired on November 2, 2006.

Synopsis

Kelly invites the entire staff to a celebration of Diwali, the Hindu Festival of Lights. Michael cheerleads the idea vigorously and reveals that he believes it to be an Indian version of Halloween.

A staff meeting is scheduled to enlighten staff members about Hindu culture. This is met with disgusted replies by Angela, excitement by Kevin (particularly after seeing illustrations in a kama sutra booklet distributed by Michael) and an uncomfortable Toby, who decides to end the meeting and takes away the booklets.

Back in Stamford, Jim has decided to follow Josh's example and ride his bike to work. Meanwhile, Andy pulls out a bottle of Jagermeister and shot glasses to turn a late night of work into a drinking game, which Karen wins by slyly pouring her shots into her wastebasket while the two men continue to down theirs.

Michael and Carol arrive at the Diwali festival in costume, since Michael thought the celebration would be a "costume party." Carol is dressed as cheerleader and Michael is wearing his papier-mâché twin from Halloween 2005, which he quickly removes.

Ryan, wearing traditional men's Indian attire, tries to get to know Kelly's family, which is met with giggling by Kelly's younger sisters, whom Ryan believes compared his looks to Zach Braff in their language (they say "Kelly likes Zach Braff... " in Hindi) and disapproval by Kelly's parents, who want to set her up with an Indian doctor. This does not get any better when Ryan tells them about his promotion at Dunder Mifflin and his plans to save money for travel and an Xbox. Dwight gets into the spirit of the festival and dons a red Kurta. Even Michael is shown dancing happily to the music.

Initially reluctant to attend the festival, Pam decides to go, ending up enjoying herself as she dances. A cleaned up Roy shows up in time to find Pam in the middle of the dancing crowd, making him wistful and awkward, and he silently exits the party.

Michael has a conversation with Kelly's parents about Hindu marriage customs and suddenly interrupts the celebration to publicly propose to Carol. Uncomfortable, Carol declines his offer and leaves the room. Michael follows her out to the car, where they briefly talk; Carol citing that this is only their ninth date, while Michael states how much he likes her. Carol drives home, leaving Michael to fend for himself and find a ride.

Meanwhile, Pam is surprised to find herself inspired by Michael's outgoing, romantic nature and she sends a text message to Jim.

However, Jim is passed out on his desk and is unaware of the incoming message on his cell phone. As the Diwali festival winds down, a dejected Michael makes an attempt to kiss a disappointed Pam, who stops him, and reluctantly agrees to drive him home, as long as he sits in the back seat. On the drive, he mentions the shoes he's wearing aren't his own.

Back in Stamford, Karen leaves for the night, as Jim continues to lie face down on his desk and Andy is laid out on the floor, both completely inebriated. Jim asks Andy if he can get a ride but Andy says "No way, dude," and breaks out an inflatable mattress. He offers to share the "roomy twin" with Jim. Jim decides to ride his bike home but barely exits the front door when he crashes sideways into the bushes. An amused Karen laughs and offers Jim a ride home. He accepts immediately and crawls into her backseat leaving her to deal with his bicycle.

Trivia

The costume Michael is wearing as he and Carol walk into the Diwali celebration was first seen in the Season 2 episode "Halloween".

This is the first time Karen's last name, Filipelli, is spoken aloud. It is mentioned by Jim as Karen walks him to her car.

Kelly's parents were played by Mindy Kaling's real parents. Kaling is Hindu in real life.

Andy's desk nameplate indicates his last name is Bernard.

During the Diwali celebration you can hear popular songs "Didi Tera Devar Deewana" (from Hum Aapke Hain Kaun) and "Ek Ladki Ko Dekha" (from 1942: A Love Story).

Michael mistakes samosas for smores.

The high school scenes were shot at the very same high school where the TV show "Freaks and Geeks" was shot. The creator of that show, Paul Feig, has directed several episodes of "The Office". Rashida Jones, who plays Karen, also appeared in one episode of "Freaks and Geeks", where she also played a character named Ka.

Memorable Quotes

Michael Scott: Nice dress, Ryan.
Kelly: It's not a dress, it's a kurtha!

Michael Scott: Tonight, one of our most ethnic co-workers, Kelly, has invited us all to a Diwali celebration put on by her community. "What is Diwali?" you may ask. Well, to have Kelly explain it, "It's, blah blah blah blah. It's so super, fun, and it's gonna be great!" Lot of gods with unpronouncable names. Twenty minutes later, you find out that it is essentially a Hindu Halloween.

Pam: [concerning the Diwali celebration] I actually might not go. Feeling kind of tired.
Meredith: Do you wanna make appletinis and watch "Sex and the City" at my place?
Pam: Oh, I don't know. I haven't decided, yet.

Pam: I just feel kind of tired, you know?
Dwight Schrute: Maybe you've got mono.
Pam: Maybe.

Michael Scott: Indians do not eat monkey brains! And if they do... sign me up! Because I am sure that they are very tasty and nutritional.

Michael Scott: It's important that this company celebrates its diversity. You know what, Stanley? Come Kwaanza time, I have got you covered, baby!
Stanley: I don't celebrate Kwaanza.
Michael Scott: Wh- Really? You should! It's fun!

Michael Scott: I love the people here, and if there's one thing I don't really care for, its that they can be terribly terribly ignorant about other cultures. And I don't want them embarrassing me in front of my girlfriend, Carol.

Kelly: Um, Diwali is awesome. And there's food, and there's gonna be dancing. And, oh, I got the raddest outfit. It has, um, sparkles-

Michael Scott: Kelly? Um, why don't you tell us a little bit about the origins of the holiday?
Kelly: Oh, um, I don't know. It's really old, I think.
Angela: How many gods do you have?
Kelly: Like hundreds, I think. Maybe more than that.
Angela: [referring to a picture of a goddess on the wall] And that blue busty gal? What's her story?
Kevin: She looks like Pam from the neck down.
Dwight Schrute: Pam wishes.

Dwight Schrute: Diwali is a celebration of the coronation of the God-king Rama, after his epic battle with Ravina, the demon-king of Lanka. It symbolizes the battle between good and evil.
Michael Scott: All right, all right. This isn't "Lord of the Rings".

Dwight Schrute: [interrupting Michael talking about M. Night Shamaylan] I see dead people.
Michael Scott: Okay! Spoiler alert!
Dwight Schrute: He was dead the whole time.
Michael Scott: Just stop it!

Jim Halpert: I started biking to work. Josh does it, and he lives a lot farther away than I do. And also, it saves gas money, keeps me in shape, helps the environment, and now I know it makes me really sweaty for work.

Michael Scott: Now, a lot of people say that Kelly is one in a million. And that's true, but it's also not true. Because, frankly, there are literally billions of people just like Kelly in the world.

Stamford Employee: Karen, my chips got stuck in the vending machine again. I need your skinny little arms.

Andy: We have such a roller coaster thing, Karen and I.
Jim Halpert: Excuse me?
Andy: Roller-coastery friendship. Hot and cold. On again, off again. Sexual tension-filled type of deal. It's very Sam and Diane.
Jim Halpert: Wow.
Andy: From "Cheers".
Jim Halpert: Yup.
Andy: Yeah.

Michael Scott: And another thing about the Indian people, they love sex positions. I present to you "The Kama Sutra". I mean look at that. Who has seen that before?
Creed: I have. That's the Union of the Monkey.
Meredith: Oh, that's what they call it!
Kevin: This is the best meeting that we have ever had.
Michael Scott: Thank you, Kevin.
Angela: You know, I find this incredibly offensive.
Michael Scott: Well, I find it beautiful.
Angela: Well, whatever Kelly wants to do in her own house is fine, but we shouldn't all be subjected to it.
Toby: Actually, she's right. This is inappropriate. Why don't I take these.
Michael Scott: No, you're not going to collect them-
Toby: Yeah...
Michael Scott: No! This is a delightful, charming culture.

Michael Scott: My Indian culture seminar was going great, until Toby decided that he was too immature to deal with culturally-explicit images. It's just sex, people! Everybody does it! I'm doing it! With Carol! Probably tonight.

Jim Halpert: Once a quarter, the sales staff at this branch has to stay late to do order form consolidation, which, amazingly, is even less interesting than it sounds.

Phyllis: Isn't this fun? Not wearing shoes?
Angela: I wish some of us still had our shoes on.
Kevin: Stop it! It's a disease! I told you!

Carol: [wearing a cheerleading outfit] I thought you said this was a costume party!
Michael Scott: [pointing out a woman] What does that look like to you?
Carol: An Indian woman in a sari!
Michael Scott: No one's even going to notice.
Kevin: Nice outfit.
Michael Scott: Hey, Kevin! It's a costume, so why don't you just cool it, okay?

Angela: [at the buffet line at the Diwali] I'm a vegetarian, what can I eat?
Indian boy: It's all vegetarian.

Angela: I'll just have some bread. [walking away after being given naan] You used your hands!

Michael Scott: [gagging] These s'mores are disgusting.
Carol: They're not s'mores, they're samosas!
Michael Scott: Do you think they have any s'mores? [cut to talking head]
Michael Scott: All they are is chocolate, graham cracker, and marshmallow. How difficult would that have been?

Pam: I decided to come. Uh, I feel a little under-dressed, but at least I'm not dressed like a slutty cheerleader, right? [pause] Is that mean?

Kelly: I don't even want to hear it, okay!? I did not come to Diwali to get yelled at!
Kelly's mom: Ryan is a temporary worker, makes no money! Wali is a whole doctor. So handsome, makes good money!
Kelly: You think I want to marry a doctor?!

Andy: Hey, Big Tuna, you ready?
Jim Halpert: Yup.
Andy: [in a Scottish accent] One, two, three, SHOT!

Michael Scott: Wow, 30 years! And two you only met once before the wedding night?
Kelly's dad: Yes!
Michael Scott: Wow.

Kelly's dad: How long have you been married to the cheerleader?
Michael Scott: Oh, she's not a cheerleader. She thought this was a costume party. Um, no, we're not married...yet.
Kelly's mom: She is very fair.
Michael Scott: She is very fair. Very fair and very kind. So, tell me, is your marriage the kind of thing where when you die, she has to throw herself on a fire? [against puzzled looks] No? Okay, but still, very cool. Okay, thanks!

Michael Scott: [to the crowd at the Diwali] Um, everyone? I'm sorry, could I have your attention please? Thank you. Hi, I'm sorry. I just have an announcement to make. Um, okay, I have learned a lot about Indian culture tonight. But I have learned even more about love. And I know your all thinking "Who is this crazy gringo and what is he talking about?" Well I'm not crazy. Maybe I'm crazy in love. So without further ado... Carol? Carol Stills? I would like you to do me the honor of making me your husband.
Carol: Oh, Michael.
Michael Scott: What do you say?
Carol: Can we talk about this in private?
Michael Scott: I didn't hear you.
Carol: [louder] Can we talk about this in private?
Michael Scott: [whispering] Oh, you've got to be kidding me. Okay. [drops microphone and walks away]

Michael Scott: Good night... Hey, you know what? Why don't I come with you? Because I've got this book, called the Kama Sutra-

Carol: Good night, Michael.

Ryan: Well, I was a temp, but I got promoted. So, um, the compensation is a lot more competitive.

Kelly's mom: So you're saving money now to start a family and home!

Ryan: Or travel, and buy an X-Box.

Pam: Can you believe my boss proposed to his girlfriend in public? That is so Michael.

Wali: Is it? He's really outgoing, huh?

Pam: Yeah. Hey, would you excuse me for a second?

Pam: It's hot in there. How's the naan?

Angela: Dry. You look like you were having fun.

Pam: I am. You should come dance with us.

Angela: I have to watch our shoes, so they don't get stolen. Who were you texting?

Pam: [quickly] No one. [cut to Jim's buzzing phone]

Karen: Andy! No a cappella!

Andy: [to Jim's singing] TUNA! ARE YOU KIDDING ME!?

Michael Scott: Pam. When Carol said no tonight, I think I finally realized how you must be feeling. We are both the victims of broken engagements.

Pam: Well, you were never really engaged.
Michael Scott: I was in that marriage arena, though.
Pam: Yeah.

Michael Scott: Yeah.
Pam: [As Michael leans in to kiss her] What are you doing?
Michael Scott: What are you doing?
Pam: I'm rejecting your kiss.
Michael Scott: [lengthy pause] Can I have a ride home?
Pam: If you sit in the back.

Jim Halpert: Hey, can I have a ride, man? I, uh, I have my bike.
Andy: No way, dude. I am not driving home. I brought an inflatable bed for just such occasions. You're welcome to share it, though. It's a roomy twin.
Jim Halpert: I'm okay.

Karen: Hey dummy! Get in the car!
Jim Halpert: I'm a drunk driver.
Karen: Yes you are.

Jim Halpert: You can really hold your liquor, by the way.
Karen: Yeah, you can't.

Michael Scott: [on the way home from Diwali] These are not my shoes.

Michael Scott: This is just like that show, "Taxi Cab Confessions".

Pam: You say one more word, I'm stopping the car.
Michael Scott: Sorry.

Michael Scott: This is going out to Indians everywhere. It's tribute to one of the greats, Mr. Adam Sandler. [singing] Diwali is a festival of lights. Let me tell you something, tonight has been one craaaaazy night! So put on your saris, it's time to celebrate Diwali! Everybody looks to jolly, but it's not Christmas its Diwali! The goddess of destruction Kali, stopped by to celebrate Diwali! Don't invite any zombies, to a celebration of Diwali! Along came Polly, so have fun at Diwali! IF you're Indian and you like to party, have a happy happy happy happy Diwali! [speaking] HAPPY DIWALI!!!!

Branch Closing

Branch Closing is the seventh episode of the third season of "The Office" (U.S. version). It was first aired on November 9, 2006. It is the first episode to have a "Producer's Cut" on NBC.com, with deleted scenes edited into the full episode and broadcast on the website.

Synopsis

Jim is using the Stamford fax machine as Karen arrives for the day and she questions what exactly he is doing. Jim says it is hard to explain. In a talking head interview, he explains that he occasionally faxes Dwight messages from "his future self" on Dwight Schrute stationery, stolen before Jim transferred. In Scranton, Dwight gets a fax saying that someone is going to poison the coffee at 8 A.M. Dwight looks up to see Stanley emerge from the break room about to take a sip of coffee. Dwight sprints to him and knocks the mug from Stanley's hand, saying that he will thank him later.

Jan Levinson enters Michael's office. He mentions he loves to start the morning with "a hearty bowl of Jan" and sings "call me Levinson in the morning" to the tune of "Angel of the Morning". Jan informs Michael that the board has voted to close the Scranton branch, adding that the board has asked her to thank Michael for his years of service. She then informs Michael that a small number of people will be transferred to Stamford while the rest will receive severance packages. Michael wants to know if he is a "small number person" or "severance" person. Jan replies that they have not made final decision on personnel yet, but adds that he will be a severance person. Michael gets extremely emotional over this news, as the rest of "The Office" stares through his window, wondering what Jan has told him. In an interview, Dwight indicates his close friendship with Michael enables him to read his mood like a book. He envisions the current title of Michael's book to be: Something Weird Is Going On: What Did Jan Say? The Michael Scott Story, by Michael Scott with Dwight Schrute.

Michael hints to "The Office" and then breaks the news prematurely and angrily, even calling Toby a "traitor" when Toby lets it slip that Jan told him minutes before Michael. Stanley says that he could not be happier, as he plans to retire and use his severance package to travel with his wife. Ryan says that it makes perfect sense that it happens today, since he has just received a box of a thousand business cards with this office address and phone number. Angela vocalizes her conviction that everyone is to blame for this. Kelly says that if she stays and Ryan loses his job, she would kill herself, like Romeo and Juliet (the Claire Danes version).

Jim thinks that it would be weird to see Scranton disappear, since he always knew that Scranton would close someday, but he just figured it would be for reason like Michael selling the building off for some magic beans. Pam thinks it is a blessing in disguise—actually not even in disguise—since she sometimes answers the phone at home with "Dunder-Mifflin, this is Pam" and now she does not have to do that anymore. Roy says he is not sure about working there if Pam is not going to be there. He says Cinderella's "Don't Know What You Got (Till It's Gone)", pretty much says what he is feeling better than he could, "in words". Ryan tells Kelly that it would not work out since they will be working separately. With the camera on him, he shows joy in how this is working out perfectly for him since he got some experience at the firm, and will get a great recommendation letter from Michael, won't have to see Kelly.

Michael and Dwight plan to confront the CFO at the New York office to talk him into changing his mind. Michael finds out in the drive that Dwight has the CFO's address on his cell phone for the Christmas card list and questions why since Dwight has never met him. Dwight replies that they will now have something to talk about when he does. They end up sitting outside the CFO's house when they are informed by the CFO's secretary that he is out of "The Office" for the day. Michael and Dwight rehearse what Michael is going to say to the CFO while they wait.

Meanwhile, Jan informs Josh that he will be taking over Dunder-Mifflin Northeast, which will be all of "The Office"s north of Stamford. However, Josh reveals that he has leveraged his new offer into a senior management position at Staples. Jim comments to the camera, "say what you would about Michael Scott, but he would never do that."

Jan tells Jim that the situation has changed. Stamford will not be closing and Scranton will be absorbing the other branch. She offers him the #2 man job at the new Northeast branch. Jim says he is unsure, as he has unresolved personal issues at the Scranton branch (which Jan assumes are due to Michael). Karen says that if asked, she would go to Scranton, and asks Jim if he will take the job at Scranton. He answers that he does not know yet, but recommends that she quit Dunder Mifflin and move to New York. As for Andy, he creates a mess in the break room when the situation changes and he learns that Stamford may be closing. Near the end of the episode, Jim reverses course, saying that he will accept the job in Scranton, and tells Karen that she should go there if offered a job. Karen then says to the camera that she is glad he said it, because even though she does not think he is into her, she is kind of into him.

Back in Scranton, Jan drops by to reveal to the rest of the staff of the change. With the exception of Stanley, "The Office" is relieved that their jobs are safe, and Pam questions Jan if anyone from Stamford will be coming back to Scranton.

Michael and Dwight wait outside the house in the car and Dwight reveals that one of his favorite moment at Scranton is Michael taking him to the hospital and telling Dwight he cared. Pam receives a rumor that Jim is coming back to Scranton and she now thinks that staying is a good thing since she doesn't have to find a new job and there is no new adjustment.

Late in the evening, Dwight checks his voicemail informing them the branch survived. The pair joyously bump chests, believing they saved the day, but unsure how they did so.

At the end of the episode, Toby said that he made plans for Costa Rica. Saying that he was dreaming of selling his house, moving, and learning how to surf, until Jan tells everyone that the branch is not closing. He says, "Costa Rica will still be there... when I'm 65."

Producer's Cuts

In subplots, Meredith seeks a potential lover based on a deal she once made to get physical with a coworker on the final day of her employment, and Creed sells off the electronics and furniture from his area of "The Office".

Meredith first believes that she made the future sexual liaison pact with Michael, but he says it is not so. Toby is equally unhelpful on the matter. Finally, Gary Trundle, Meredith's former coworker from another branch's warehouse, calls to remind her of a deal he had made with her long ago. Meredith plans a rendezvous at her place in 20 minutes. She confirms the closing to Gary even after she knows that the decision to close has been reversed.

Dwight searches through the CFO's garbage outside his home, learning that he is rich (as he has a satellite TV bill) and drinks coffee, "possibly to disguise the smell of cocaine".

Jim's line about his theory that Scranton would close "because Michael sold the building for magic beans" is changed to an awkward high school reunion that ends up with everyone moving in with him.

Andy asks Jim what he's going to do if he should get laid off. When Jim asks Andy, he says that Cornell has a great alumni network and he might go back there to teach. Jim then asks where he went to college, mocking Andy's frequent reference to his alma mater.

In an extended scene, we find out that Ryan and Kelly's relationship may be more than it seems. Kelly appears to have a strange power over Ryan. He claims he "can't explain" the attraction and why they remain together.

Creed takes pictures of office property on his desk and advertises the items online. He makes several deals throughout the day and ultimately earns $1,200 selling Dunder-Mifflin property from a branch now scheduled to remain open.

A Guide to "The Office": Season Three

Trivia

There is only one Sal's Pizza in Scranton and their order menu is posted in "The Office" kitchen, which would indicate "The Office" is possibly close to 505 Linden St.

During Michael's talking head segments, Steve Carell does not blink.

Michael mentions the movie "Kingpin" when he and Dwight first approach the front door of the CFO's house. In the movie, an older Roy Munson (Woody Harrelson) lives in a run-down Scranton apartment. The movie portrays Scranton rather insultingly, making it interesting that Michael enjoys the movie.

When Kevin tells Pam that they are going to Poor Richard's, he mentions that Creed will be buying shots. This is most likely because Creed had just made $1200 selling electronics from "The Office", however, the original cut of the episode does not show that plot line and causes the statement to be slightly out of context.

At the end of the show, when Michael and Dwight are sitting in front of the house, there appears to be lights on upstairs, and the porch light is also on.

Currently, castmember Jenna Fischer thinks this episode is "the best one we've ever done. I'm not kidding", according to her Myspace blog.

Memorable Quotes

Dwight Schrute: When you become close with someone, you develop a kind of sixth sense. You can read their moods like a book. And right now, the title of Michael's book is.. "Something Weird Is Going On...colon...What Did Jan Say? The Michael Scott Story...by Michael Scott. With Dwight Schrute."
Jan: I am here to tell you that we are closing the Scranton branch.

Michael Scott: I don't understand.
Jan: The board voted last night to close your branch.
Michael Scott: On whom's authority?
Jan: The board's.

Jan: A small number of people will be transferred to the Stamford branch, and the rest will be getting severance packages.
Michael Scott: Am I a small number person or a severance package person?
Jan: Well, we haven't made final decisions about personnel yet...but you're a severance package person.

Jan: Our CFO believes that Josh is going to play an important role in our company's future.
Michael Scott: Oh really, what role is that? King of the stupid universe?

Michael Scott: It is an outrage, that's all. They're making a huge, huge mistake. Let's see Josh replace these people. Let's see Josh find another Stanley. You think Stanleys grow on trees? Well they don't. There is no Stanley tree. Do you think the world is crawling with Phyllises? Show me that farm. With Phyllises and Kevins sprouting up all over the place. Ripe for the plucking. [long pause] Show me that farm.

Michael Scott: [trying to delicately break the news to his staff] It's over. We are screwed. Dunder Mifflin Scranton is being shut down.

Jim Halpert: I don't have a ton of contact with the Scranton branch, but before I left, I took a box of Dwight's stationery, so from time to time I send Dwight faxes. From himself. From the future. [reading fax] "Dwight, at 8am today, someone poisons the coffee. Do not drink the coffee. More instructions will follow. Cordially, Future Dwight."
[Dwight receives the fax and reads it. He spots Stanley about to drink a cup of coffee]
Dwight Schrute: Noooooooooo! [smacks the cup out of Stanley's hands] You'll thank me later.

The Merger

The Merger is the eighth episode of the third season of "The Office" (U.S. version). It aired on November 16, 2006, as a special 40-minute episode.

Synopsis.

Pam congratulates Toby on a road race, but Dwight questions the true value of the accomplishment and claims that he could finish a mile faster on a skateboard. He brags that he outran a black pepper snake just last week and comments in an interview that his speed falls between that of "a snake and a mongoose ... and a panther." Outside, Dwight stretches to prepare for his run around the building in his suit and dress shoes. Pam is assigned to time him, but she admits that her "timer" is a digital thermometer, and excuses herself back inside.

In Stamford, "The Office" is being packed up in anticipation of the move to Scranton. Jim high-fives Karen and briefly wears a paper hat reading "Stamford R.I.P." made by Andy, and a stack of the hats are seen in a recycling bin. Andy questions Jim about his new supervisor, Michael Scott, but Jim plays it close to the chest. Andy threatens to crush Jim if he gets in his way and rolls away a PC from Josh Porter's office.

Pam returns with two paper grocery bags full of supplies to which Michael instructs her to arrange the conference room "as though you are trying to impress an older man way out of your league." In an interview she professes enthusiasm and excitement regarding the merger of Stamford employees into the Scranton branch, including the Jim's return.

Kevin is told to shred the company documents from Stamford, which he relishes in doing. As he demonstrates the power of his shredder from Staples, Kevin gets carried away and accidentally shreds his credit card. As Michael is putting nameplates on the desks for the new people, Dwight suggests that they fire Tony Gardner to consolidate power. In an interview, Dwight says that he would have been good as the Japanese soldier who chose which prisoner to execute once a new batch of prisoners arrived.

In a parking lot interview next to his Nissan Xterra, Andy proclaims he'll be the No. 2 man in Scranton in six weeks time through "name repetition, personality mirroring and never breaking off a handshake". Indeed, he echoes Michael's "Aloha" greeting and refers to his "nifty gifty" bag, which contains mostly pencils and coupons to local Scranton "hot spots". Meanwhile, Dwight instructs Jim not to mess with him, as he is older and wiser. Jim gapes at Dwight's forehead, freaking him out.

Dwight introduces himself to Andy and each man believes the other will be reporting to him in the revised office hierarchy. Andy mentions that his title contains the word 'director' which outranks a 'manager' on a film set. He proceeds to question Dwight to ascertain what he knows about film. Dwight states he knows everything about film since he has seen over 240 films.

Jim goes over to say "hi" to Toby, and is then somewhat confused when Toby asks him to pound it.

An elated Kelly hugs Jim and informs him there is a lot she must catch him up on, and proceeds to tell him about the babies Tom Cruise and Katie Holmes and Brad Pitt and Angelina Jolie had. Jim then asks Kelly what's new with her and she replies, "I just told you."

Michael plans an orientation in the "banquet room", but stops Meredith from drinking champagne, and beseeches Kelly not to eat the snacks, telling her to treat it like beef. When informed she eats beef, he says to treat it like poisoned beef, because the snacks are for guests. In a familiar manner, Karen gives Jim a stick of gum and Pam notices somewhat disapprovingly. Michael plays a videotape he has created called "Lazy Scranton" featuring himself and Dwight rhyming over the music of Saturday Night Live's "Lazy Sunday". Jim says the video treat reminds him of his orientation film: "The Scranton Witch Project." The viewer is shown a brief clip of that film, which features Michael illuminated by a flashlight saying he "gets so scared when people don't label their personal food." While it is obvious that everyone is bored, Michael says that he thought the video would be an "A" or an "A+"; then, he remembered that there is an "A++".

In the coffee room, Pam notes that Jim has purchased a bottle of water from the vending machine instead of grape soda that he used to frequently purchase while at Scranton. Jim simply replies "I'm evolving, Pam." which to note, his sleeves are buttoned up.

Pam then questions when Jim is going to tell her everything and if he is interested to go for a coffee after work. Jim replies not tonight since he is still settling in and then Michael walks in the room, making things even more awkward.

In a series of vignettes, Stamford transplants are distracted by their new Scranton coworkers: Ryan by Hannah's open use of a breast pump; Karen by Phyllis's perfume from metropolitan Orlando; Martin by Creed's feet-up, boisterous phone conversation. In an interview, Stanley questions the audacity of "these new people" and mentions he's silently sat downwind from Phyllis's stinky perfume for years.

The integration portion of Michael's orientation finds four new employees sitting in chair on the banquet room table. The boss and Dwight try to force hefty, skeptical Tony up on the table, and he quits instead. Jan later calls Michael and yells at him for firing Tony when he tried to quit (an impulsive decision Michael made after feeling insulted by Tony's attempt). She complains that because Michael fired Tony rather than letting him quit like he wanted to, Dunder Mifflin has to pay him severance. Michael initially uses Dwight as a scapegoat by saying "Bad advice from my number two." of which Jan corrects him and says Jim is actually going to be the number two. This is eventually brought into a meeting between Michael, Dwight, Jim and Andy and culminates in yet another battle between Dwight and Andy for Michael's respect.

After Tony leaves the room, Hannah walks out, agreeing Michael is unprofessional. A short while later, Michael runs to the conference room and tells everyone to go down to the parking lot because someone has let the air out of all their tires. The employees rush down to see what is going on and Michael blames Bob Vance Refrigeration employees. Martin notes Michael's tires remain fully inflated, but Michael says he was left an evil note under his windshield wipers reading, "You guys suck! You can never pull together as one and revenge us. That is why you suck!" Michael suggests stealing all of the refrigerators from Bob Vance in retribution. Everyone shakes their heads in disbelief at what Michael has done. Once again, Pam noticed Karen causally touching Jim's back with her hand as they walk away. Later, all the employees are shown talking to each other and getting along due to a common interest: Michael as an unprofessional boss. Michael watches from his office and comments how a common enemy has brought the Stamford and Scranton employees together, although he apparently believes that the employees have fallen for his scheme and consider Vance Refrigeration the common enemy, not Michael himself.

Jim sits in his Toyota Corolla and receives a call from Karen, requesting that they meet up. He quickly ends the conversation as he sees Pam and runs over to say the day had been awkward and that he feels he should tell her he is seeing someone. She denies awkwardness and states that they'll always be friends.

Kevin uses the shredder to make a salad. Dwight and Andy trade numerous barbs on a downward elevator ride. Andy disses

Dwight's Trans Am, which is defended as classic American muscle. Andy praises his luxurious, rugged, Japanese Xterra, but Dwight says the vehicle's name isn't even a word and makes little sense.

Trivia

"The Daily Show" correspondents Ed Helms and Steve Carell reunite in this episode. Incidentally, Helms took over many of Carell's segments on the Daily Show after Carell left.

This episode references Saturday Night Live twice: Michael's orientation film parodies "Lazy Sunday" and Michael and Andy perform Haddaway's "What Is Love" and other elements of A Night at the Roxbury.

Michael misattributes the question "Can't we all just get along?" to "the Reverend King" when it was actually stated by Rodney King.

Andy takes over Oscar's desk, as the character is purportedly taking a three-month company-sponsored vacation with his roommate, Gil. Actor Oscar Nunez is currently filming a pilot for Comedy Central.

Staples paid to place a red-and-white-logo shredder in the episode, with scenes of Kevin using and praising it before accidentally shredding his own credit card with it. A web page on

Staples website was set up to denote the appearance of the shredder on the show as well as a cast autographed unit is to be auctioned on eBay with proceeds benefiting Boys and Girls Clubs of America. In the show, Staples is the main competitor of Dunder-Mifflin and has been mentioned numerous times including in "The Convention" and "Branch Closing". The actual shredders have the logo stamped on outer metal shell of the shredder only with no color.

Hooters received yet another mention in "The Secret".

The version of this episode available for purchase on iTunes is missing both scenes featuring Kevin and his paper shredder, most likely because the Staples product placement agreement may not have included distributable episodes.

An unknown character is present in the conference room during the "Night at the Roxbury" scene, and is later on seen sitting next to Andy when Dwight tells Michael to fire Andy.

Memorable Quotes

Dwight Schrute: What was your mile time?
Toby: About seven.
Dwight Schrute: I could beat that on a skateboard.
Toby: Well, that has wheels.
Dwight Schrute: Yeah, well, my feet don't. And I could still crush that time.

Michael Scott: My branch is absorbing the Stamford branch. Or as I like to put it, my family is doubling in size.

Dwight Schrute: The Japanese camp guards of World War Two always chose one man to kill whenever a batch of new prisoners arrived. I always wondered how they chose the man who was to die. I think I would have been good at choosing the person.

Michael Scott: [To Martin Nash, who is black] Follow me, I will show you where all the slaves work. Uh, not...

Dwight Schrute: Hello. I don't believe we've been introduced. Dwight Schrute, Assistant Regional Manager.
Andy: Andy Bernard, Regional Director in charge of sales.
Dwight Schrute: So you'll be reporting to me then.
Andy: On the contrary.
Dwight Schrute: My title has "manager" in it.
Andy: And I'm a director. Which on a film set, is the highest title there is. Do you know anything about film?

Dwight Schrute: I know everything about film. I've seen over 240 of them.

Andy: Congratulations.

Michael Scott: This is an orientation, not a bore-ientation.

Karen: Does Bob Vance work for Vance Refrigeration?

Jim Halpert: Does he ever.

Michael Scott: [reading threatening note that he actually wrote]: "You guys suck! You can never pull together as one and revenge us. That is why you suck!"

icon
The Convict

This is the ninth episode of the third season of "The Office" (U.S. version). It aired on November 30, 2006. It was written by Ricky Gervais and Stephen Merchant, who created the original version of "The Office".

Synopsis

Hannah Smoteridge-Barr brings her infant son to work where his all-pink ensemble causes some confusion as to his gender. The baby is met with ambivalence from Stanley's and Creed's attempts to play a paperclip-based game against Karen's advice. Michael can't help himself, and crawls under a nearby desk to act as the voice of the child riffing on lines from the "Look Who's Talking" film series.

Angela, Kevin, Michael and Pam teleconference with Jan in order to determine the origin of a rebate check "The Office" received. Jan informs the group the check stems from a federal reformed convict employment program, a "smart move" by Josh Porter, former manager of Dunder-Mifflin Stamford. She e-mails human resources and quickly determines the employee hired through the program is one Martin Nash.

Michael proposes that the four of them forget the news they've received to avoid creating problems among employees. All agree, although Michael fails to note the sarcasm in Angela's voice when she says she supports protecting a criminal, especially as a "90 lb. female who sits in a poorly-lit, rarely-visited corner of "The Office"".

Meanwhile, Andy dials Jim's extension and whispers "I'm horny". Jim is astounded but soon realizes Andy wants the inside scoop on his female coworkers and asks for a debriefing on Kelly, Angela and Pam. Jim encourages Andy to pursue Pam and, as a prank, coaches him on her favorite things; In actuality, his tips are things that Pam dislikes or has no opinion on: Disc golf, pig Latin, and the Six Flags television commercial "with the old guy".

Dwight assures Michael he is of a collected, cool mindset to hear a piece of news that he may not necessarily approve of, but when he learns of Martin's criminal past, he attempts to sprint away. In an interview he says he simply doesn't like criminals. Michael himself announces Martin's "problems with Johnny Law" to everyone, and says that for every trusted white man, he can name a black man he trusts more. He then asks employees to call out names of white men. He tops Pam's father with "Danny Glover", but is unfamiliar with Jim's suggestion of "Jonas Salk"; Jim quickly substitutes Justin Timberlake, which garners "Colin Powell". Karen suggests "Jesus", to which the boss replies "Apollo Creed" to which Stanley simply rolls his eyes in casual disbelief.

In the break room over lunch, Martin tells the others he was incarcerated for insider trading, and although it was routine and could be dull, he enjoyed certain perks of prison, including outside time and art classes. Ryan is told about prison business classes taught by Harvard Business School guys. Pam comments that prison sounds better than their current work situation and Kevin wonders why the branch doesn't receive daily outdoors time.

Soon, Michael announces an hour of outdoors time will take place in the parking lot. Nearly everyone heads outside to bitter cold temperatures. Michael offers a weightlifting session with a 2.5 lb. dumbbell he produces from the trunk of his Sebring, but a freezing Stanley leads a charge back into the warmth of "The Office".

Michael soon calls an impromptu meeting in which he dons a do-rag and attempts to "scare you straight" as an ex-con character named "Prison Mike". He speaks with a New York accent, calls Angela a bee-yoch, threatens to shove her up against a wall (and incites Dwight to politely come to her defense with the rest of the staff), says life "in the clink" is no picnic, alludes to violence and rape and singles out Ryan because, in prison, he would be "da belle of da ball", who responds "Michael, please." in discomfort.

Jim asks Prison Mike where he learned so much information about the country's correctional system, and he claims it's a mix of the Internet and prison. Jim asks his crime and Angela is peeved when Dwight asks Prison Mike the worst thing about prison, which he responds by claiming there were Dementors. Andy plays along, and says prison sounds awful. Prison Mike concludes his speech, saying "You got a good life." Martin comments that Michael's performance did not remind him of his time in prison. A frustrated Michael locks everyone in the conference room, who become concerned and begin moving around for an exit. Hannah, still at her desk with the pink-clothed child, ignores Kevin's pleas for assistance.

Pam phones Toby who tells Michael the staff is fully aware a workplace is better than prison and are simply teasing him. A relieved Michael releases his prisoners, including Stanley who never stopped work on his crossword puzzle through the entire incarceration. Martin, who apparently didn't find these antics particularly funny, cleans out his desk and quits Dunder-Mifflin. In his office, Michael remarks to the camera that he thinks Martin is a quitter.

In the last few moments of the episode, Andy strums "The Rainbow Connection" on his banjo, while singing pig Latin in his "sexy, high, falsetto voice" in an attempt to woo Pam based on Jim's advice. She smiles politely and glances at Jim, who gives the camera his trademark smirk.

A Guide to "The Office": Season Three

Trivia

Michael attempts to tune a television in the break room playing a fuzzy WBRE-TV broadcast featuring weather forecaster/chief meteorologist Josh Hodell.

Prison Mike is modeled after the 1978 documentary Scared Straight!.

The earliest president's son that "Prison Mike" could have kidnapped is George H.W. Bush, or, depending on how old he was when he did it, one of the sons of Jimmy Carter, as President Clinton and George W. Bush have daughters.

During the scene where Michael Scott is Prison Mike and talks about the dementors, it is clear that John Krasinski (Jim) is caught laughing for real at Steve Carrell's antics as he looks into camera all red faced and can hardly control himself.

Ed Helms showcases his real ability to play the banjo.

"Dementors" are the guardians of the prison in the Harry Potter series of books.

Memorable Quotes

Jim Halpert: [picking up phone] Jim Halpert.
Andy: I am so horny.

Jim Halpert: Okay, I can't help you with that.

Andy: Oh, I think you can, Big Tuna. Tell me about that Indian chick, Kelly. She seems pretty slutty. Good for a romp in the sack.

Jim Halpert: She is dating Ryan, I think.

Andy: Oh, and I care why?

Jim Halpert: She's high-maintenance.

Andy: Next. How about...[sees Meredith walk by] Angela. Blondes are more fun. C'mon, trust me on that.

Jim Halpert: Yeah, trust me, that would be fun for no one.

Michael Scott: I didn't hire an ex-convict. Unless they mean Toby. Convicted rapist.

Michael Scott: Why did the convict have to be a black guy? It is such a stereotype. I just wish Josh had made a more progressive choice. Like a white guy. Who went to prison for...polluting a black guy's lake.

Angela: Sure. Let's protect the convicts. At the expense of the general feeling of safety in the workplace. As a 90-pound female that sits in an ill-lit, rarely-visited corner of "The Office", naturally I agree with that.

Dwight Schrute: I am greatly concerned about having a convict in "The Office". And I do not care if that convict is white, black, Asian, German, or some kind of halfsy. I do not like criminals.

Andy: I live to frolf.

Kevin: I had Martin explain to me three times what he got arrested for, because...it sounds an awful lot like what I do here...every day.

Jim Halpert: Quick question — do you play the guitar?
Andy: I play the banjo.
Jim Halpert: Hold on, let me think about that...yes, that'll work. But can you sing in a sexy high falsetto voice?
Andy: [singing] You know I can, my man.

Michael Scott: [to Ryan during a "scared straight" seminar] You, my friend, would be da belle of da ball.

A Benihana Christmas

This is the tenth episode of the third season of the US version of "The Office". It originally aired on December 14, 2006, and was directed by Harold Ramis, who has helmed movies such as "Caddyshack" and "Groundhog Day".

Synopsis

It is the day of the annual office Christmas party at Dunder-Mifflin Scranton. Dwight enters "The Office" with a goose that he accidentally struck with his car, which he proclaims to be a Christmas miracle, and announces his plans to prepare it for feasting during the party. After initial objections to having a dead animal present, Toby allows Dwight to keep it as long as he cleans it in his car.

When Michael arrives, we see Pam give him a gift bag. He mistakenly thinks it's from Pam but she explains it's from corporate headquarters.

Carol receives her Christmas card from Michael and visits him to voice her disapproval of his Photoshopping his head onto the body of her husband, as pictured in a two-year-old ski weekend family photo with her, the ex-husband, and the kids. This, along with his marriage proposal, pushes her over the edge, and she breaks off the relationship, leaving Michael (who has already booked a trip for the two of them to Sandals Resorts) heartbroken. Michael opens his gift from corporate and finds it is a Dunder-Mifflin bathrobe, which he promptly dons for comfort from his break-up.

Pam gives Jim her gift: she has been sending fake messages to Dwight from the CIA for several months (including a request of Dwight to admit all the secrets he's sworn never to tell anyone) and she's going to let Jim decide the top secret mission that Dwight will go on. At first, Jim is clearly happy, but then turns down the offer, saying that he doesn't want to keep doing the same things he did before now that he is "Number #2" man in the branch and he has a chance to start over. Pam is obviously embarrassed and saddened that Jim turned down her gift.

Dwight realizes that "The Office" is short one bathrobe, and a depressed Michael "solves" the problem by telling Dwight to take Toby's.

Angela and the rest of "The Office"'s party planning committee gather to figure out the specifics about the day's holiday-oriented activities. Karen attempts to offer several party suggestions, which Angela immediately vetoes. Karen is then asked to leave by Angela for having stupid ideas, and does so after receiving no support from the other committee members.

Later, after stating to the camera that she does not know why she has been so mean to Karen, Pam apologizes and the they decide to organize their own Margarita-Karaoke party. When they present this idea to Angela, she declares their committee to be invalid and asks Dwight get involved since he "outranks" Karen and Pam. Jim, being "Number #2", creates a "Validation Committee" (consisting only of himself) and declares Pam and Karen's committee to be valid. As this goes on, Andy decides to take Michael out to help him forget about his troubles. Michael summons his "entourage" Jim, Ryan and Dwight to come along, though Ryan opts out with a long list of excuses he's prepared for such an invitation from Michael.

Pam and Karen begin their party in the break room and Angela (after calling Dwight for permission) is quick to start her own in the conference room. Stanley goes to Pam and Karen's party. Several other people follow him except for Kevin, Phyllis, and Hannah. Kevin tells the camera that he is mainly convinced to go because he has heard that Angela's party will have double-fudge brownies, and that cancels out the fact that Angela herself will be there. Michael, Andy, Jim, and Dwight arrive at a Benihana restaurant (which Michael believes at first to be "Asian Hooters"). Andy slides into a seat next to Michael and arranges the seating so Dwight is on the opposite end of the table and out of earshot of the conversation of the rest of the group. Andy convinces Michael to ask out his Japanese waitress after getting him slightly drunk.

Meanwhile, "The Office" is divided into two separate camps as Phyllis, Hannah and Kevin attend Angela's party while the rest of the staff are at Pam and Karen's. Ryan makes the discovery at the party that they do not have a power cord for their karaoke machine, but Darryl offers to get his synthesizer as an alternative. As he passes Phyllis to get the music out of his car, she asks him how they are doing over there and Darryl replies that they are having fun, encouraging Phyllis to join their party in the break room "when your meeting is over". Through Karen and Pam's party, Meredith is seen with a bottle of vodka in her hand, turning down the margaritas because they are "too sweet".

Angela's party proceeds to get more uncomfortable as Angela makes a dig at Kevin's weight, irritating him enough to drive him to the other party. When Michael, Andy, Jim, and Dwight return with two of the waitresses from Benihana, Michael finds Angela's party to be "lame." Kevin uses this moment to escape. Angela is comforted by Dwight's attendance at her party until Karen and Pam come in and tell Dwight that he's won the raffle from their party. Dwight wins walkie-talkies, which he uses later in the episode to communicate with Angela, using their pet names for one another, "monkey" and "possum".

Pam notices how upset Angela is, and she and Karen make an offer to Angela to merge the two parties. Angela agrees and reveals that she stole the power cord for the karaoke machine. As everyone has fun singing, Michael—who is very drunk—confuses his date with Andy's since, as he states, "all waitresses look alike." This confusion continues until he identifies his date and marks her arm with a marker.

The two waitresses leave because they say the party "blows", and Michael offers his girl a trip to Sandals Jamaica, where he was going to take Carol. She turns down the offer since she has school, although she does accept a bike that Michael had intended to give to the charity toy drive.

A depressed Michael sulks on the couch until Jim comes up and joins him. Jim gets Michael to laugh at the whole situation and lets him realize that what he had with the waitress was nothing more than a rebound. Jim then tells Michael that a rebound is a fun distraction, but when it is over, "you're still thinking about the girl you're really after—the one who broke your heart" (echoing Jim's relationship with Karen after his being rejected by Pam). The two sit in silence as they muse over this.

As the Christmas party winds down, Angela sings karaoke, Pam finds a way to get Toby a robe from corporate, and Jim and Karen give each other the same Christmas gift (a DVD copy of "Bridget Jones: The Edge of Reason"), much to Pam's disappointment. Later Pam receives a gift from Roy, which Jim sees. Michael makes a phone call to an unknown person to ask him or her to accompany him to Sandals; to Michael's surprise, the person says yes. Oscar and Gil return from their three-month vacation in Europe. Looking around, Oscar says "Too soon" and leaves.

While Jim is leaving, he decides to go ahead and take Pam up on her "gift" offer from earlier. He tells Pam that Dwight will be summoned by the CIA to meet with them. Pam quickly looks up how much a bus ticket will cost, and when she mentions it will cost $75, Jim tells her that the CIA will be sending a helicopter instead. The next scene shows Dwight on the roof waiting for a helicopter. He then receives a text message that says the mission has been compromised and he must abort it and destroy his phone, which he promptly does by throwing it from the roof.

Trivia

The two Asian waitresses at Benihana are not the same two waitresses Michael and Andy bring back to "The Office". According to the propmaster of the show's blog, the reason for the different actresses was because Andy and Michael failed to pick up the original waitresses, and all they could get were "less attractive ones".

In real life, the closest Benihana location to Scranton, Pennsylvania is over ninety minutes driving away. Therefore, it would have been unlikely for the characters to leave "The Office", eat at Benihana, and return to the Scranton branch in three hours, as suggested by the episode's dialogue.

Being the first hour long episode in the show's history "A Benihana Christmas" was counted as two episodes in the 25 episode third season.

The Benihana restaurant set used in this episode looks similar to the set used for the Benihana scene in "The 40-Year-Old Virgin", also starring Steve Carell. In fact, Carell's characters in both "The Office" and "The 40-Year-Old Virgin" are sitting in the same seat at the restaurant tables.

In a deleted subplot, Kelly thinks Ryan did not get her a Christmas present. She then reveals that she threw out her gift to Ryan, leading Ryan and Kelly to dumpster dive outside.

Dwight adding drum noise with his mouth during Angela's karaoke version of "Little Drummer Boy" is a reference to a scene of the "Pilot" episode, in which he annoys Jim with the same song.

This is the third time in the series that a word has been bleeped (when Michael rides his bicycle into a potted plant in the first scene after the credits).

This episode marks the return of Oscar Martinez, who has not appeared since the first episode of the third season due to his three months paid vacation offer by Corporate as an apology.

In "The Alliance", Angela claimed that green is whorish. In this episode, she now believes that orange is whorish. Her decision on what is whorish appears to correspond with Phyllis' outfits.

When Angela discusses her estranged sister, she says "so, yeah... I'm pretty good." This is what Kevin says when talking about his success at the World Series of Poker in the Season 2 finale "Casino Night".

Creed is seen in the first scene with Toby, Dwight and Phyllis. Yet after the opening credits, he is seen entering "The Office" for the first time, then stealing a gift, which Jim criticizes him about.

A Guide to "The Office": Season Three

Memorable Quotes

Dwight Schrute: [bringing in a dead goose] I accidentally ran over it. It's a Christmas miracle!

Dwight Schrute: He was already dead, and we Schrutes use every part of the goose. The meat has a delicious smoky rich flavor. Plus, you can use the molten goose grease and save it in the refrigerator, thus saving you a trip to the store for a can of expensive goose grease.
Jim Halpert: Wow. Win-win.
Dwight Schrute: Exactly, thank you, Jim.
Phyllis: I like goose. If it's already dead, is it so crazy if we eat it?
Creed: That's crazy. It's crazy.

Michael Scott: Hey! I would like a nice slice of Christmas Pam. Side of candy Pams. And perhaps some Pam chops. With mint...
Pam: Can I help you, Michael?

Jim Halpert: It's a bold move to Photoshop yourself into a picture with your girlfriend and her kids on a ski trip with their real father. But then again, Michael's a bold guy. Is bold the right word?

Michael Scott: I'd like everybody's attention. Christmas is canceled.
Stanley: You can't cancel a holiday.
Michael Scott: Give it up Stanley or you'll lose New Year's.

Stanley: What's that mean?

Michael Scott: Jim, take New Year's away from Stanley.

[Michael is laying behind the reception desk, we only see his legs sticking out from it.]

Michael Scott: It hurts my heart. It hurts my stomach. It hurts my arms.

Pam: Okay, well why are you laying like that?

Karen: Uh, so I had a couple of ideas to make the Stamford people feel more at home. Each year we have a Christmas raffle...

Angela: It would never work here.

Karen: Okay...um, another idea was karaoke...

Angela: No.

Karen: A Christmas drinking game...

Meredith: YES.

Angela: God help you!

Ryan Howard: I miss the days when there was only one party I didn't want to go to.

Dwight Schrute: Pam and Karen! I am ordering you to cease and desist all party planning immediately.

Pam: You can't do that.

Dwight Schrute: As ranking number 3 in this office, I am ordering you to-

Andy: Ummm, I'm number 3.

Dwight Schrute: You're number 4.

Andy: Yeah, but I'm number 3.

Dwight Schrute: Uh, no. You must turn over to me all Christmas decorations and party paraphernalia immediately. They will be returned to you on January 4th.
Jim Halpert: Okay, I think I can help here.
Dwight Schrute: Okay good, they...
Jim Halpert: As ranking number 2, I am starting a committee to determine the validity of the two committees and I am the sole member of the committee. We'll act on this now.
Dwight Schrute: Okay, this is stupid.
Jim Halpert: Can you please keep it down? I'm in session. [thinks] I've determined this committee is valid.
Dwight Schrute: No, no, no. Wait. Permission to join the Validity Committee?
Jim Halpert: [thinks about it] Permission denied.
Dwight Schrute: Dammit!

Michael Scott: I need my entourage. Jim, Dwight, Ryan, c'mon - we're going to Asian Hooters.
Ryan Howard: I'm not feeling so well. I've got a ton of work to do here. MSG allergy, peanut allergy, I just ate there last night.
Michael Scott: [feels Ryan's head] Alright, feel better.
Jim Halpert: Wow, thanks for taking all the excuses, dude.
Ryan Howard: Doctor appointment, car trouble, plantar warts, granddad fought in World War II. Use your head, man. I keep mine in here [shows Blackberry]. Look alive, Halpert. Welcome back.

Michael Scott: Bros before hoes. Why? Because your bros are always there for you. They got your back after your ho rips your heart out for no good reason. And you were nothing but great to your ho, and you told her that she was the only ho for you. And that she was better than all the other hoes in the world. And then suddenly...she's not yo' ho no mo'.

Back from Vacation

Back From Vacation is the eleventh episode of the third season of the US version of "The Office". It aired on January 4, 2007, and was the first episode to air after the winter hiatus.

Synopsis

Jim is presiding over a meeting with Karen, Dwight, Phyllis, Stanley, Ryan, and Andy. After Jim notices Dwight with a tape recorder, Dwight explains to Jim that while Michael is away on vacation he is to record and type up the transcript of every meeting that occurs. Jim jokes loudly to the recorder that Dwight is "completely nude and is holding a plastic knife to Stanley's neck," The other workers (except for Stanley and Ryan) begin to tease Dwight jokingly with similarly outlandish false statements. The scene ends after Andy shouts "I am now chopping off Phyllis' head with a chainsaw".

Michael returns from his Jamaican holiday rejuvenated, unfazed by the news that Hannah quit and filed a complaint against the company while he was away. Michael directs the Party Planning Committee to throw a luau-themed party in the warehouse to coincide with the postponed annual inventory project that evening. The committee initially objects to the last minute nature of this party. Michael attempts to impart the lessons of his vacation, displaying to the staff a photograph of a sign in Jamaica reading: "no shirt, no shoes, no problem". An astounded

Pam notices Jan Levinson in the margins of the photo and points it out to her colleagues. Michael states to the camera that Jan didn't want anyone to know they traveled together since it may get them both in trouble. He then reveals he and Jan had an affair in Jamaica.

Despite half-hearted attempts to keep this information under wraps, the photo is soon forwarded to the entire office. A fearful Michael attempts damage control, avoiding Jan's phone calls and dodging inquiries from Toby.

Karen is upset with Jim as he has expressed objections to the idea of Karen moving into an apartment two blocks away. When Pam asks Jim what is wrong, Jim reveals that he and Karen have been dating for a month and argues that living on the same street might be "a little close." Pam convinces Jim that he is being unreasonable and persuades him to apologize to Karen. During the luau, Jim hands Karen a note. Karen is pleased, asking Jim, "Are you sure?"

During inventory, Dwight walks in on Pam crying in private. Though Dwight appears to have good intentions, handing Pam a handkerchief and trying to comfort her, he mistakes Pam's crying for PMS.

As the luau/inventory is held, Jan arrives at "The Office" to speak with Michael in private. Without explicitly revealing whether or not she is aware of the image being sent throughout the email system, she confesses her attraction to him against all reason.

She informs Michael that on her psychiatrist's advice, she has decided to give in to her self-destructive tendencies and continue their affair. She kisses Michael and instructs him to make an excuse to leave "The Office" party so he can meet her at his condo. In a reference to the movie "Jerry Maguire", Michael tells Jan, "You complete me." Jan looks pained for a moment, and leaves.

Back in the warehouse, Pam and Roy joke about their failed engagement and Kevin takes home a large poster printout of the oversized vacation photograph produced earlier by warehouse personnel, stating that he will hang it at home since he doesn't have a lot of art.

Trivia

During a break room chat between Pam and Jim, Pam says she endured listening to Michael play a conch shell, though he only is shown playing a steel drum.

Ed Helms only had an hour of lesson time before playing the drums

The object that Darryl finds is an iPod dock with speakers.

When exiting the warehouse after seeing the photo poster, Michael and Dwight take a left after stepping out of the doorway, when in the next clip they clearly have taken a right out of the doorway.

As of this episode, only two people (Andy & Karen) from the Stamford branch remain at the Scranton office.

Memorable Quotes

Michael Scott: Hey Mon!
Pam: Hey, you have a bunch of messages...and that's nice. Hanna quit while you were gone. I guess she memo 'd a file some complaints she had about being a working mother, and so you might also have to be deposed.
Michael Scott: Blah, blah, blah, blah, blah, blah, blah.. relax, just relax. Ok, I'll get to all of it later.
Pam: It's kind of serious.
Michael Scott: Aren't you going to ask me how Jamaica was? Say it... ask me.
Pam: How was Jamaica?
Michael Scott: It was sooo good! Awwwwwh! Hey mon! At Sandals, Jamaica, when somebody says "Hey Mon!" everyone says "Hey Mon!" back.
Stanley: Oh Michael, I'm glad you're here.
Michael Scott: Stanley, you know what, it is really good to see you too.
Stanley: My bonus check was $100 less than you promised.
Michael Scott: Ok, well then Payroll is in charge of all of that.
Stanley: They said I should to talk to you.
Michael Scott: Well, I'm just getting settled in, so I'm gonna...

Stanley: I am not doing a lick more work till I get my full bonus check.

Michael Scott: You are not as much fun as your Jamaican brothas... mon.

Michael Scott: You know I had never been out of the country before now. Got to see how Jamaicans live, it is great, you know, they just relax, they party all the time.

Pam: It's kind of an impoverished country.

Michael Scott: Yeah, gosh, great. You know what Pam, make a note... I want us all to start having Pina Coladas everyday at three.

Pam: You can't today, we're doing inventory.

Michael Scott: Inventory is at the end of December.

Pam: We couldn't do it without you so we postponed.

Michael Scott: I specifically went on vacation so I would miss it.

Michael Scott: Inventory is boring. In the islands they don't make you do stuff like take inventory. Why do think so many businesses moved to the Caymans?

Michael Scott: Tonight we are going to have an inventory luau. I want to bring back a little slice of paradise to the Dunder-Mifflin warehouse inventory, so party-planning committee, get on it.

Angela: By the end of the day? That's impossible.

Michael Scott: The Jamaicans don't have a word for "impossible."

Jim Halpert: Yep, it's English, it's "impossible."

Michael Scott: How hard is a luau? All you need is some grass skirts, pineapple, poi, tiki torches, suckling pig, some fire dancers. That's all you need.

Michael Scott: Jan told me to play it cool and not tell anybody because it could get us both in trouble. So officially I did not see her. But I did see Jan there. In our room. At night, and in the morning. That's all I'm gonna say. We had sex. We had sex. I had sex with her. I had sex with Jan.

Michael Scott: Daryl! Hi, where's Daryl?
Roy: He's in "The Office".
Michael Scott: Hi. Hey, man... how's it going?
Darryl: Alright, what's up Mike?
Michael Scott: That's great. Ok, umm, so did you get an e-mail from me?
Darryl: Yeah.
Michael Scott: Ok, well that was supposed to go to Packer, not Packaging. Did you already forward it to a whole bunch of people?
Darryl: Uh huh.
Michael Scott: Ok. Well, did you get the second e-mail that I sent? Explaining that the first e-mail was a mistake and that you should delete it...
Darryl: Yep
Michael Scott: And you sent that out to everyone?
Daryl [eating lunch]: Michael, I'm very busy down here.

Michael Scott: I have a special assignment for you.

Dwight Schrute: Who's the target?

Michael Scott: A sensitive e-mail has been released to "The Office". It contains a file, a picture, the filename is jamaica-jan-sun-princess.

Dwight Schrute: What's it of?

Michael Scott: Not important.

Dwight Schrute: I'm not sure, you need to tell me everything or I cannot accept this assignment.

Michael Scott: Ok. Forget it.

Dwight Schrute: Ok, I accept it.

Pam: Dunder-Mifflin, this is Pam. Just a second. Michael, it's Jan on the phone.

Michael Scott: Oh God, no, no, no... Pam. Pam. Tell her I'm not here. Tell her I ran out of gas... hit a deer... I hit a deer with my car. Tell her I hit a cat. I hit a cat.

Pam: He'll call you back.

Michael Scott: She bought it? Ok, Ok.

Dwight Schrute: Michael hit a deer?

Pam [crying by herself}

Dwight Schrute [enters hallway]: Who did this to you? Where is he?

Pam: What, no it's nothing.

Dwight Schrute [takes off jacket, ties it around his waste]: It's hot in here.

Pam: Yeah.

Dwight Schrute: Yeah. [give Pam handkerchief]

Pam: Thanks, you don't need to stay here.

Dwight Schrute: I know. [puts arm around Pam]

Pam [continues crying]

Dwight Schrute: So you're PMS'ing pretty bad, huh?

Pam [cries more]

Jan: You're wrong for me... in... in every way. But I still find myself wanting to be with you.

Michael Scott: And I to you... in addition, feel, the same feelings, that you are, as well.

Jan: Good. Good.

Michael Scott: So, um, thanks for coming by.

Kevin Malone [folding up poster of Michael and Jan]: What am I gonna do? I'm going to hang it up at home. I don't have a lot of art.

A Guide to "The Office": Season Three

Traveling Salesman

Traveling Salesman is the twelfth episode of the third season of the US version of "The Office". It aired January 11, 2007, and is the seventh episode directed by series show runner Greg Daniels.

Synopsis

Michael dresses the rear of his flat screen computer monitor with novelty teeth, a tiny Fez and Post-It eyes and commands it to say rude things to Jim and Pam via a text-to-speech application on his computer.

Meanwhile, Kevin informs Angela that the corporate office has yet to receive important tax documents and warns Angela that if she forgot to send them in, "it is a big deal." Angela appears troubled. Later, Dwight is seen arriving at "The Office", where Angela has intently perched herself near reception. Angela asks if everything is okay, and Dwight informs her that she "is in the clear." Angela is visibly relieved.

Dwight, however, is late to Michael's "dream team" sales meeting, prompting taunts from Andy Bernard regarding his tardiness. Michael informs them that at Andy's suggestion, they'll be pairing up for sales-call duty. Given first choice, Andy selects Michael. Phyllis, whom Michael refers to as "our resident senior" picks Karen. Told he cannot select "pass", Stanley selects Ryan. Dwight is angered when he is left to partner with Jim.

Michael tosses a bag of laundry to Dwight who in turn throws it into his Trans Am. Michael dubs the sales calls "The Amazing Race" even though there will be no winner, and a prize will not be awarded for the largest sale. To supplement his statement, he assigns each pair a nickname based on previous contenders from Race. Michael dubs Stanley and Ryan "the retired Marines", Phyllis and Karen "mother and daughter", Jim and Dwight "the gay couple", and his own team "the firefighter heroes". Before heading out, Michael snatches Phyllis's car keys from her hand and tosses them underneath her vehicle. Upon the team's departure, Angela invites Pam for coffee.

Andy, riding shotgun in Michael's convertible, continually bags on Dwight, using every attempt to sway Michael's opinion him. He becomes frustrated, however, as Michael casually deflects his suggestions. Andy asks Michael why Dwight does his laundry. Michael explains that Dwight's laundry duty is punishment for attempting to take Michael's job in a secret meeting with Jan.

At the sales call, Michael's attempt to sell the small-town personal feel of Dunder-Mifflin is thwarted as Andy interrupts with tales of his privileged upbringing and boasting of the company's listing on the New York Stock Exchange. Afterward Andy apologizes for losing the sale, informing Michael that he really "screwed that up... I really Schruted it".

Meanwhile, while en route, Ryan asks Stanley if he can take the lead on the sales call, and Stanley happily accepts. The pair meet with four African American men in the lobby of their business, one of whom knows Stanley. Ryan, flustered, is unable to mutter anything but "Hi. Hi. Hi. Hi." Later Stanley mocks Ryan for his ineptitude, comparing his behavior to that of his six-month-old niece.

Before Jim and Dwight depart, Jim reveals to the camera that he and Dwight used to frequently go on sales calls in the past. Dwight sits in the rear driver's-side seat of Jim's Saab. At the sales meeting, the pair enact a tag-team sales routine, wherein Dwight borrows a phone and works his way through the call center of what he says is a competing paper company and is put on hold for several minutes while Jim dials Dunder-Mifflin customer service and Kelly answers immediately and amicably. A sale is quickly made.

Rather than immediately head out on their call, Phyllis drives Karen to a nearby beauty salon and purchases a beauty treatment she describes as "makeovers" for the pair. At their sales call, a large sale is quickly procured. Karen is impressed with Phyllis' savvy, as it is revealed through a photograph on the client's desk that his wife subscribes to a similar beauty sensibility. Later, Phyllis mentions her happiness for Karen and Jim's relationship as she had worried he would never overcome his crush on Pam, inadvertently revealing its existence to Karen.

At a coffee shop, Angela tells Pam a thinly-veiled story of her friend "Noelle", who missed a deadline to send in important documents to corporate in New York and the "gallant gentleman", "Kurt" who drove the documents all the way to New York and handed them in for her. Pam seems to see through the charade, however.

Upon their return, Karen invites Jim to coffee where he assures her that his crush on Pam has passed and that he is glad that Karen moved to Scranton. Meanwhile, Andy steals Dwight's car keys and searches his car, yielding a tollbooth receipt from a trip that morning to New York. Proffering the stolen ticket as evidence, Andy's suggestions finally begin to take hold as Michael is coaxed into believing that Dwight has gone behind his back to the corporate office, betraying him again. After confirming with Jan that Dwight was present at corporate that morning, Michael approaches him with Andy in tow, demanding an explanation. Dwight refuses to acknowledge or explain his presence at the corporate office, but assures Michael that has not betrayed him. Michael insists on an explanation by the end of the day, implying that Dwight may be fired if he does not comply with his request.

Dwight and Angela consult. Dwight will have to choose between betraying Angela by making their relationship public, or betraying Michael by withholding information about his whereabouts that morning. Shortly after, Dwight stands up at his desk, requests the attention of "The Office" and announces his resignation:

" Although I love this company more than almost anything in the world, I have decided to step down from my post and spend more time with my family. I do not fear the unknown. I will meet my new challenges head-on, and I will succeed, and I will laugh in the faces of those who doubt me. It's been a pleasure working with some of you, and I will not forget those of you soon. But remember, while today it is me, we all shall fall. In other words, I'm quitting. "

He bequeaths his box of desk items to Michael, but keeps two bobblehead dolls, including the likeness of himself. On his way out, Dwight approaches and embraces Jim who is walking with Karen through the parking lot. They are unaware of his resignation since they were both at coffee at the time. Andy gloats to the camera about his clever plan to get rid of Dwight while Angela vengefully glares at Andy from the background, suspicious that he's responsible for Dwight's resignation.

Trivia

While Michael is typing "Long time. Me lobe yoy long time", the screen shows that Michael had also typed "Pam is the receptionist", which is never heard from the computer during the scene before.

The executive Jim and Dwight meet with tells them he caught a fish on Lake Wallenpaupack, the real northeastern Pennsylvania lake that was the site of the "Booze Cruise" episode.

When Angela is talking to Pam while getting coffee she refers to a hypothetical situation involving Noelle and Kurt. In "Conflict Resolution" and "The Injury", it is revealed that Dwight's middle name is Kurt. It is therefore a reasonable assumption that Angela's middle name is Noelle.

Phyllis states she's glad Karen has entered Jim's life to help him get over Pam; however, in "Branch Closing", she tells Pam excitedly of overhearing Jim was to return from the Stamford branch.

Dwight's farewell salute was first seen in the episode "Initiation".

This is the first episode of the series to use a new, shorter title sequence. The new title sequence has been used in all subsequent episodes.

Memorable Quotes

Harvey: I am Harvey, a computer. Jim sucks.
Harvey: Me so horny. Me love you long tim.
Pam: Who's Long Tim?
Harvey: Long time. Me lobe yoy long time.
Jim Halpert: Well Yoy should bring Long Tim in someday
Harvey: You ruined a funny joke, get out of my offive.

Ryan Howard: I'm very flattered. I was his second choice, after "pass"

Michael Scott: Fool me once, strike one. Fool me twice, strike three.

Jan: And where it asks to state your business he wrote, "Beeswax, Not Yours, Inc." [After Karen has had a makeover]
Karen: Hey, you wanna get a coffee?
Jim Halpert: Sure. Who are you?

Jim Halpert: Ah, young Jim. There's just so much I need to warn you about. And yet, tragically, I cannot.

Pam: Angela, you seem so happy. I bet you wish you were like this all the time.

Andy: I really Schruted it.

Dwight Schrute: Here's my card. It's got my cell number, my pager number, my home number, and my other pager number. I never take vacations, I never get sick, and I don't celebrate any major holidays.

Michael Scott: I want you to think about it long and hard.
Dwight Schrute: That's what she said.
Michael Scott: (lowly) Don't you dare.

Dwight Schrute: Although I love this company more than almost anything in the world, I have decided to step down from my post and spend more time with my family. I do not fear the unknown. I will meet my new challenges head-on, and I will succeed, and I will laugh in the faces of those who doubt me. It's been a pleasure working with some of you, and I will not forget those of you soon. But remember, while today it is me, we all shall fall. In other words, I'm quitting.

Andy: Oompa loompa, doompadee dawesome, Dwight is now gone, which is totally awesome. Why was he gone, he was such a nice guy. No, he was not, he was a total douche. Doompadee doom.

Ryan Howard: Dwight will be missed. Not by me so much...but he will be missed.

Dwight Schrute: One of my life goals was to die right here, in my desk chair. And today, that dream was shattered.

Jim Halpert: After you
Dwight Schrute: No thank you, I never let anyone walk in front of me
Jim Halpert: How come?
Dwight Schrute: 7 out of 10 attacks come from the rear
Jim Halpert: That still leaves 3 out of 10 attacks that could come from the front
Dwight Schrute: But I would block the attack, rendering it-
(Jim slaps him)

The Return

This is the thirteenth episode of the third season of the US version of "The Office". It aired on January 18, 2007, and marked the return to work of Oscar Martinez, who had been on vacation since the first episode of the third season.

Synopsis

Dwight schedules some job interviews, including one where he offers his prospective employer a three volume résumé consisting of his professional career, the second, his athletic history, and the third of Dwight Schrute trivia. At another interview, when asked to describe himself in "three words", Dwight offers: "Hardworking. Alpha male. Jackhammer. Merciless. Insatiable..." Dwight settles for a job at Staples to earn money while he continues his job search.

Andy is irritating his coworkers tremendously, including Michael, who is growing weary of Andy's incessant badgering and brown-nosing. He has relocated to Dwight's former desk where he severely irritates Jim and Ryan, whom he attempts to nickname "Big Turkey". Andy casts an invisible fishing line in an pantomimed attempt to hook Jim (the "Big Tuna"), and calls his own cell phone in order to demonstrate his new self-recorded ringtone, "Rockin' Robin" in four-part harmony (all four parts sung by himself.) He also repeatedly sings one portion of The

Cranberries song "Zombie" in his falsetto voice, going flat several times in the process.

Oscar returns after his paid vacation and Kevin asks him how he enjoyed his "gay-cation", stating that he devised the joke shortly after Oscar left and has been saving it. Angela invites Oscar to join the party planning committee. At first he is offended, but Angela respectfully continues to ask, explaining that "certain events have transpired", and apologizing for the way those events transpired. She breaks into tears explaining how she "would just like to make some changes about certain things and certain situations and certain accountants..." Oscar quickly accepts, reassuring her.

Michael welcomes Oscar by asking the party planning committee to have a Mexican-themed fiesta celebrating his return, offending Oscar in the process. The committee outfits "The Office" with numerous piñatas and Ryan uses a marker to change the spelling on the bottle of lemonade to read "Lemoñadé."

Jim tries to enlist Karen's help in pulling a prank on Andy, but she is busy with the influx of clients that she inherited upon Dwight's departure, stating that Dwight's files are password-protected with the names of different mythical creatures. Ryan too gruffly refuses to join in the hi-jinx, much to Jim's dismay. Finally, Jim approaches Pam, who readily agrees. Jim steals Andy's cell phone and hands it off to Pam. Pam hands it back to Jim in the break room and stands guard as Jim pushes up a ceiling tile and launches the phone through the empty space, atop a tile roughly above Andy's desk. Karen briefly notices the actions of the two. The pair trade off placing calls to Andy's phone, frustrating him until he eventually accuses Phyllis of stealing it.

Andy, still jubilant that Dwight is gone, continues sucking up to Michael. Due to Andy's pursuit of "face time" with his boss, Michael begins avoiding him, stating that Andy is "annoying the bejesus" out of him.

Angela reveals to Michael that the reason Dwight visited the corporate office was to deliver her tax documents, noting that no other employee — Andy in particular — would have done so. Andy offers to hang out with Michael, but Michael declines, requesting that Andy cease and desist his annoying behavior. Michael's rejection of Andy's offered friendship, combined with Pam and Jim's prank, pushes Andy over the edge and he punches a hole in a wall, shocking his co-workers. Michael leaves "The Office" to try to get Dwight back.

Michael finds Dwight working at Staples and admits to him that he was wrong, and tells Dwight that if he would go out of his way for a "random co-worker", he had misjudged him from the beginning. Michael apologizes, and asks Dwight to return to "The Office". Dwight accepts Michael's apology, asks not to do Michael's laundry anymore (Michael is non-committal), and returns to "The Office" in a daze, finding his co-workers celebrating Oscar's welcome back party, which he thinks is being held for him.

At the party, Karen observes Pam and Jim laughing together about the prank. She confronts Jim, asking him if he still has feelings for Pam. After several seconds of silence, Jim nods and answers "Yes". Karen stands up and walks out, visibly upset.

Dwight is handed a broom and blindfold to break open a piñata. Declining the blindfold, he knocks the piñata to the ground and begins pummeling it into shards. He triumphantly continues throughout "The Office", decimating the decorative piñatas hung from the ceiling as he goes. Andy sulks in the break room. Michael states that he prefers being sucked up to for reasons of love rather than career advancement.

Trivia

Like "Branch Closing", an extended version of "The Return" appeared on NBC.com and the iTunes Store, featuring several deleted and extended scenes, including:

Michael's convertible top has mechanical problems and will not go up. Michael advises Oscar to "put rainbow stickers on the back". Michael comments on the "German engineering" of Oscar's Lexus RX. In a talking head interview, Oscar admits that he is not sure whether he wants everyone to "just keep their mouth shut" about his orientation, or keep going "because I could use a home theater system".

Oscar runs into Creed and Jim in the kitchen and asks them where Dwight is, prompting Creed to describe events from "Grief Counseling" (completely unrelated to Dwight's departure). Jim, being at Stamford at that time, says he is sure none of that's real, causing Creed to shout "You're not real, man!"

Brief shot of snow collecting in Michael's uncovered convertible.

Kelly is surprised that Oscar has never heard of Lance Bass, and advises Oscar to "learn more about his culture."

Michael asks Jim what he thinks of Andy. Michael claims on paper that he and Andy should be best friends. Jim tells him that the Andy will only say what makes Michael happy, being a "yes man". Michael doesn't understand what this means until Jim tells him that Andy did the same thing with Josh.

In a talking head interview, Michael recalls a childhood memory of being put to bed in Spider-Man pajamas and his mother kissing him on his butt accidentally. Thus he knows what it is like to have your butt kissed literally, saying "and it better not be what Andy is doing".

Angela confides in Pam about missing Dwight. She tells Pam she doesn't want people to know about their relationship. Pam tells her there has to be a way she can get Dwight back without spilling the beans. Angela claims she cannot, as she is "not like Pam, walking around in [her] provocative outfits, saying whatever thought pops in [her] head".

Michael states in an interview that he made a big mistake replacing Dwight with Andy, a person who "loves the company so much he punched a hole in it".

Michael's search for Dwight in Staples is extended.

Creed asks Meredith to draw him a map to the aisle where she bought one of the snacks. Referring to her as "Mama", it is not clear if he loves the food or hates it.

Michael shakes maracas at Pam while saying "I will shake mine, and then you will shake yours." Pam promptly says "No I will not". Phyllis proceeds to shake her chest enthusiastically, causing Pam to smile and Michael to walk away in defeat.

Michael asks Oscar if this party reminds him of his childhood, Oscar says it reminds him of the movie "¡Three Amigos!". Michael is flattered by Oscar's suggestion and takes it as a compliment.

The episode ends with Andy driving to a ten-week Anger Management program he has been ordered to attend. Andy prefers to think of it as "Management Training." He tells the documentary crew that he intends to complete the program in five weeks by employing a strategy of "name repetition, personality mirroring, and positive reinforcement through nods and smiles," similar to the strategy announced upon his arrival at

Scranton. Andy claims "I'll be back, just like Rambo" as he greets his counselor.

NBC Entertainment President Kevin Reilly played Dwight's first interviewer. Reilly was a strong supporter of "The Office" during its first season despite low ratings.

The shirt that Dwight wears upon return to "The Office" has the "Battlestar Galactica" logo on it, the second reference to the 2004 reimaging of Galactica during the series.

While asking Michael if he wanted to 'hang out' for "T.G.I. Wednesday", Andy says he can't wait to "go home and get his beer on and get his "Lost" on".

The Dwight "rescue" from Staples by Michael emulates the ending of "An Officer and a Gentleman" by playing a muzak version of "Up Where We Belong" in the background.

Jim says he misses Dwight the episode when Oscar returned, and Dwight sarcastically said he missed Jim in episode when Oscar left in "Gay Witch Hunt".

Memorable Quotes

Michael Scott: I don't want somebody sucking up to me because they think I am going to help their career. I want them sucking up to me because they genuinely love me.

Andy: [To Michael] I forgot to tell you the plan for this Saturday. You, me, bar, beers, buzzed. Wings, shots, drunk! Waitresses - hot! Football, Cornell-Hofstra, slaughter! Then quick nap at my place, then we hit the tizzown.

Dwight Schrute: How would I describe myself? Three words - hardworking, alpha male, jackhammer. Merciless. Insatiable.

Jim Halpert: I miss Dwight. Congratulations, universe. You win.

A Guide to "The Office": Season Three

Ben Franklin

Ben Franklin is the fourteenth episode of the third season of the US version of "The Office". It aired on February 1, 2007. It was written by Mindy Kaling and directed by series cinematographer Randall Einhorn.

Synopsis

The episode opens with Michael attempting to film a video to be presented at the event of his death to his future unborn son.

Michael has planned two separate parties for Phyllis and Bob Vance to celebrate their upcoming wedding. Michael announces Phyllis' wedding in six days, and declares that he is "instituting Prima Nocte." Jim remembers the term from the movie "Braveheart", and confirms the meaning of Michael's confusing statement on Wikipedia, revealing that it refers to the ancient right of kings to deflower every new virgin in his kingdom on her wedding night. Michael then apologizes for making the statement.

Pam notices that Jim is tired, and Jim states in a talking-head interview that Karen and he have been talking about their relationship for the past five nights.

Todd Packer arrives and, true to form, accuses Jim of being gay. In trying to hit on Karen, he is shocked to learn that she is Jim's girlfriend. Packer is insulted that Michael has not ordered a stripper for the bachelor party that Michael is organizing for Bob Vance. Michael can't because of potential sexual harassment issues, but Packer tells him that getting a male stripper for Phyllis' party as well as a female one for the bachelor party makes it all OK.

Michael leaves it up to Dwight and Jim to organize two strippers, male and female, for the parties. While Dwight successfully locates a stripper for Bob Vance's party, Jim decides to undermine Michael's enthusiasm and orders a male scholastic speaker instead.

Michael and Ryan visit a sex shop for party favors. Michael is overwhelmed, and Ryan states, "he hasn't even said a word yet ... just giggling". Upon their return, The Scholastic speaker arrives. It is Benjamin Franklin, and Michael, under the impression that he's a male stripper, asks if he's wearing a thong. "Ben Franklin" is introduced to the women (with Michael laboring under the impression that Ben Franklin was a US President), and Pam and Karen have fun interacting with the character.

Outside the warehouse, Michael grills steaks on the same George Foreman grill that he once burned his foot on but tells Ryan not to worry as he has cleaned all the foot off of it. Inside, Kevin attempts to organize a game of professional poker, while Michael advertises his steaks as "man-meat". Dwight says enthusiastically that he wants some of Michael's man-meat.

While joking about Ben Franklin in the break room, Karen tells Pam that she knows about her past relationship with Jim. Pam is startled, and asks what Karen means. Karen tells Pam she knows that she and Jim had kissed in the past, and that it's not a big deal, as "it's just a kiss". Karen asks Pam if she's still interested in Jim, to which Pam absently replies "oh yeah." Karen is startled, but Pam states that she misunderstood what Karen had asked, and tells Karen that she should proceed with her relationship with Jim.

The female stripper arrives, in character as an office secretary. Roy claims in a talking-head that's he's "not really into strippers," but that he finds secretaries to be sexy. As Bob Vance refuses a lap-dance, Michael volunteers. The dance proceeds for a short while before Michael brings it to a halt, stating that his girlfriend might object.

Dwight makes the now-fully-clothed exotic dancer, Elizabeth, answer phone calls in "The Office", because he has already paid her for three hours of work. She compliments a clearly distressed Angela on a baby poster nearby.

Michael goes to the stripper for advice as to whether he should tell Jan about his lap-dance. She replies, "secret secrets are no fun, secret secrets hurt someone". Dwight claims that he is ninety-nine percent sure that the impersonator is not the real Ben Franklin, "no matter what Jim says!".

"Ben Franklin" reveals to Pam that his real name is Gordon in an attempt to hit on her. He also advises Michael to keep the lap dance a secret. Michael calls him a sleaze-bag. He calls Jan out of a meeting to confess to her the lap dance. A frustrated Jan tells him she's closer to firing him than dumping him. Michael seems to take this as good news.

Pam and Jim have a understated confrontation in the break room which ends with Pam telling Ryan she's ready for him to set her up with some of his business school buddies, in front of a visibly shocked Jim. Dwight grills Ben Franklin on his revolutionary-era knowledge, and Michael reflects that Ben Franklin turned out to be a creep while the stripper turned out to give great advice ... advice that rhymed.

Trivia

Oscar does not appear in this episode, despite returning in the previous episode, "The Return". Andy also does not appear, as he is in anger management training.

Toby also does not appear due to the fact that he was "sent home by Michael" so he wouldn't know of the strippers. This was shown in the deleted scenes for the show.

Ryan asks Michael if the grill at the bachelor party was the same one he cooked his foot on (and it was), which happened in the episode "The Injury".

The stripper compliments Angela on her baby poster that she received from Toby in the "Christmas Party".

The Benjamin Franklin impersonator, Gordon, was portrayed by actor Andrew Daly.

The blouse worn by the stripper during the party is a previous "Pam shirt" according to Jenna Fischer's MySpace blog.

Memorable Quotes

Michael Scott: Yesterday I was scraping some gunk off my wall sockets with a metal fork and I gave myself the nastiest shock. When I came to, I had an epiphery. Life is precious and if I die, I want my son to know the dealio. The dealio of life.

Michael Scott: So I am instituting "prima nocte."
Jim Halpert: [talking head] "Prima nocte", I believe from the movie "Braveheart" and confirmed on Wikipedia, is when the king got to deflower every new bride on her wedding night. So...
Michael Scott: I'm sorry, I had a very different understanding as to what "prima nocte" meant.

Todd Packer: Mike, okay, a stripper is "Bachelor Party 101." If you don't get a stripper your party is gonna suck.
Michael Scott: I can't get a stripper here. Sexual harassment.
Todd Packer: Get one for the girls, too. That evens it out. You know, separate but equal.
Michael Scott: So that's what that means...

Michael Scott: Okay, coed naked strippers in this office. For realsies.

Angela: Under no circumstance should a man strip off his clothes in this office.

Meredith: SHUT UP, ANGELA!

Dwight Schrute: (ordering stripper) Ruddy cheeks, thick calves, no tats, no moles. No tats. No, TATS. Of course I want t-

Jim Halpert: Stop. That's disgusting.

Dwight Schrute: Leave me alone and get the male stripper.

Jim Halpert: Fine.

Dwight Schrute: I knew you would, Nancy.

Jim Halpert: Sally.

Jim Halpert: Michael referred me to a male strip club called "Banana Slings." Instead, I called the Scholastic Speakers of Pennsylvania.

Michael Scott: Mr. Franklin, I would say you are probably one of the sexiest presidents ever.

Ben Franklin: Well, actually, I never was president.

Michael Scott: Yes, but Ben Franklin was.

Dwight Schrute: I don't care what Jim says, that is not the real Ben Franklin. I am 99% sure.

Ben Franklin: You know, I invented electricity.

Pam: I know.

Ben Franklin: Well, I'm sensing a little electricity right here.

Pam: Didn't Ben Franklin have syphilis?

Ben Franklin: Yes, but I don't. My name is Gordon.

Pam: Oooh...

Michael Scott: So you know who turned out to be kind of a creep? Ben Franklin.

Michael Scott: Guys! Beef: it's what's for dinner! Who wants some man meat?

Dwight Schrute: I do! I want some man meat!

Jim Halpert: Michael, Dwight would like your man meat.

Michael Scott: Well then, my man meat he shall have.

Phyllis' Wedding

This is the fifteenth episode of the third season of "The Office". It was written by Caroline Williams and directed by Ken Whittingham.

Synopsis

Jim, who has spent several weeks conditioning Dwight to want a mint when he hears the Window's unlock workstation sound, restarts his computer and gives Dwight an Altoid.

Michael announces that he will be co-giving away the bride at Phyllis' wedding, as he has been charged with pushing her father's wheelchair down the aisle. Phyllis confides in her colleagues that she invited Michael to be a part of the wedding party in order to secure six weeks off, a first for the branch.

Michael plays a video of the last wedding he attended- that of his mother to his stepfather when he was ten. In the video, the young Michael wets his pants and tells his stepfather he hates him before running off. The ring is then strapped to a dog, who urinates all over the church.

The wedding invitations, as it turns out, are almost exactly like the wedding invites Pam had sent out for her cancelled wedding. Even the letters P and R are present on the invite, and in the same font.

In the church, Dwight is suspicious of the robust turnout and appoints himself to act as bouncer so as to eject any wedding crashers or uninvited guests.

Michael approaches Phyllis, farts, and advises her to cover the bald spot. He also lets her know that he vomited, and she's welcome to do so as well if she's nervous.

Kevin expresses suspicion that Toby met his attractive date at the gym and Meredith scolds Kelly for wearing white to the wedding. As Phyllis enters the church for her walk down the aisle, Pam exclaims "That's my dress!"

Phyllis then walks down the aisle rather quickly, forcing Michael to do some fairly impressive and quick maneuvering with her father in the wheelchair. He runs the chair over the hem of Phyllis' dress and then her father puts the brakes on, and gets up to walk his daughter to the podium. Michael, feeling upstaged, neglects to unlock the chair, dragging it to the front and elbowing his way into the line of groomsmen.

Mid-ceremony, Creed arrives and places his card on a gift from another guest, discarding the original card into the circular file.

At the reception, Dwight evicts a man who first identifies himself as Uncle Al, but then fails to recall the name of the couple.

Shortly thereafter, the band makes an announcement before beginning their set: Uncle Al is missing, and he is "old, with brown eyes and dementia." The next shot is of Uncle Al venturing into the street and then shuffling back to the safety of the curb.

Elsewhere, Pam tells Roy that Phyllis used all of Pam's wedding plans for her own ceremony and reception. Roy didn't notice as he wasn't terribly involved in the planning of their cancelled nuptials.

During the toasts, Michael takes it upon himself to make a speech. He accidentally reads the definition of "welding" instead of "wedding" and says the couple are like gold medals. After telling the crowd Phyllis' high school nickname— "Easy Rider" — Bob Vance throws Michael out. He later tries to sneak back in but Dwight refuses to authorize him to do so.

Pam and Jim dance just before the bouquet is tossed. Ryan deflects the bouquet away from Kelly into the hands of Toby's date.

Later, Roy pays the band $20 to play Jewel's "You Were Meant for Me" and asks Pam to dance. They do so and then leave together, prompting Jim to express his enthusiasm for his own date, who is belting out an off key rendition of a Police song.

Michael is then re-admitted into the ceremony when he arrives with Uncle Al, whom he found outside.

Memorable Quotes

Michael Scott: Phyllis is getting married and I am in the wedding party. She has asked me to push her father's wheelchair down the aisle, so basically I am co-giving away the bride. Since I pay her salary it is like I am paying for the wedding, which I am happy to do. It's a big day for Phyllis, but it's an even bigger day for me - Employer-of-the-bride.

Phyllis: Yes, I put Michael in my wedding. It was the only way I could think of to get six weeks off for my honeymoon. No one else has ever gotten six weeks before.

Dwight Schrute: The Schrutes have their own traditions. We usually marry standing in our own graves. Makes the funerals very romantic, but the weddings are a bleak affair.

Michael Scott: Phyllis, did you break wind?

Michael Scott: Me walking Phyllis down the aisle was supposed to be the highlight of the wedding. And now, the wedding has no highlight.

Minister: And do you, Bob Vance of Vance Refrigeration...

Michael Scott: If you ever lay a finger on Phyllis, I will kill you.
Bob Vance: If you ever lay a finger on Phyllis, I'll kill you.
Michael Scott: Agreed. No fingers will be laid on Phyllis.

Kelly: Are you all right? This must be so awful for you.
Pam: What do you mean?
Kelly: Well, this was supposed to be your wedding.
Pam: Oh, um, no, that's, um, it's actually fine.
Kelly: There's no way it's fine, I'm sorry. If I was you, I would just like freak out, and get really drunk, and then tell someone I was pregnant.

Michael Scott: The Merriam-Webster dictionary defines wedding as, "The fusing of two metals.

Business School

This is the sixteenth episode of the third season of "The Office". It was written by Brent Forrester and directed by Joss Whedon.

Synopsis

Michael happily announces that he will be a "special lecturer emeritus" in Ryan's emerging enterprises class. In his talking head interview, however, Ryan seems sort of ambivalent about bringing Michael—it will bolster his grade in the class, however, Michael is….Michael. Michael, in his own talking head, compares himself to a "cool" teacher from his childhood who actually happened to be a pedophile.

To prepare for his lecture, Michael asks Dwight what was the most inspiring thing he has said to him. Dwight immediately says: "Don't be an idiot." In an interview, Dwight explains that whenever he is about to make a decision, he asks himself "Would an idiot do that? And if they would, I do not do that thing."

In another part of "The Office", Roy tells Pam that he can't wait for Pam's art show. She is now dating Roy again and Jim summarizes the situation with: "Pam's with Roy, I'm with Karen, Brangelina's with Frangelina."

Michael arrives at Ryan's campus and after watching a group of students play frisbee, exclaims that he wants to get his "friz on." He then barges into the game and tosses the frisbee into the distance.

They arrive at the classroom and Ryan characterizes Dunder Mifflin as a dying company. Michael, who couldn't hear him, enters with bragadoccio, playing a Brandenburg concerto on a boombox. He opens his speech by ripping the pages out of a student's expensive textbook, and throws candy bars at the students in an attempt to illustrate the challenges in starting one's own business. He then instructs the students to take down the phrase "real business is done on paper."

A question and answer session follows Michael's main presentation. Students ask how Dunder Mifflin can compete with the "five Goliaths" of the paper industry. Michael says that the students are just too young and too inexperienced to understand the business world. He also states that the United States faces "five goliaths" and lists four: Al-Qaeda, Global Warming, sex predators, and mercury poisoning. One of Ryan's colleagues reveals that Ryan considers the company a sinking ship, and Michael tells the student that Ryan still hasn't made a sale, started a fire in his attempt to make a cheese pita, and "a lot of people think he's a tease." He then leaves, shouting, "Ryan doesn't know anything, and neither do any of you. So suck on that!"

In the car ride home, Michael tells Ryan to clean out his desk. He will be moved to the annex... right next to Kelly. Michael explains this move by saying that "... a good manager doesn't fire people, he hires people and inspires people... people will never go out of business".

At "The Office", Dwight notices something suspicious on the floor and concludes that a bird is stuck in the vent. He goes to liberate it, and a bat flies out. The staff panics and Dwight shuts the bat in a conference room. Angela puts on a clear plastic rain bonnet so the bat won't defecate on her head.

Jim and Karen then tell Dwight that they were bitten by the bat and may turn into vampires at any moment. Dwight doesn't quite buy it.

Dwight later decides to trap the bat and ends up trapping Meredith's head in a bag along with it. He manages to liberate Meredith and releases the bat into the open.

At the art show, Roy appears with his brother and makes a point to remind Pam that none of her coworkers are there. Roy quickly leaves with his brother and tells Pam to come to his place when he's done. Oscar's boyfriend, Gil, says that her work is little more than overpriced hotel paintings, but at the end of the night, Michael arrives and is impressed with her work. He buys a picture to hang in "The Office" and she is noticeably touched.

Trivia

The following scenes were deleted:

In the kitchen area, Karen starts to pull down a flier posted for Pam's art show, but stops when Oscar enters.

Creed has some papers for Phyllis and decides to wait at her desk to give them to her even though she won't return from her honeymoon for six weeks.

Stanley proclaims he will have six weeks in paradise too, with Phyllis on her honeymoon. He moves a stack of his own papers to her desk.

While trapped in the bathroom Meredith shouts, "I really want to come out." Dwight suggests she "light a match."

While leaving, Angela tells Kelly this is what happens with the power of prayer. Kelly asks her if she prayed for the bat incident. Angela says "in a general sense."

During a talking head interview, Dwight asks, "What is a leader?" Jim says he's heard of a ladder but not a leader.

Michael explains to the students that if they had a sticker business, they would need to sell the stickers for more than they paid for them.

Michael is asked by a business school student, "How much of Dunder Mifflin's profits are put back into research and development?" Michael tells the student that the question is Gobbledegook.

Memorable Quotes

Michael Scott: A boss is like a teacher. And I am like the cool teacher. Like Mr. Handell. Mr. Handell would hang out with us. And he would tell us awesome jokes. And he actually hooked up with one of the students. Um, and then like twelve other kids came forward. It was in all the papers. Really ruined eighth grade for us.

Ryan Howard: If you bring your boss to class, it automatically bumps you up a full letter grade. So I'd be stupid not to do it...right?

Dwight Schrute: If a vampire bat was in the U.S., it would make sense for it to come to a "-sylvania." Like Pennsylvania.

Michael Scott: There are four kinds of business. Tourism. Food service. Railroads. And sales. And hospitals/manufacturing. And air travel.

Michael Scott: [using candy bars of the same name to illustrate his point] You need something to sell. Now this could be anything. It could be a thingamajig. Or a whosi-whatsi. Or... ...a "Whatchamacallit."

Now, you need to sell those in order to have a "PayDay."
And, if you sell enough of them, you will make a "100 Grand."
[takes out a 100 Grand candy bar and throws it to the students. It hits a student in the face.]
Satisfied?

A Guide to "The Office": Season Three

Cocktails

This is the seventeenth episode of the third season of "The Office". It was written by Paul Lieberstein and directed by JJ Abrams.

Synopsis

Dwight helps Michael get into a straightjacket wrapped in chains for a magic demonstration. As Michael prepares, Jim and Pam make sure that all present understand that Michael is to receive no help in his escape, no matter what he says. After brief struggling, a key falls out of Michael's mouth. Jim covers it with his foot and Michael hops to his office. He closes the blinds with his feet and wiggles around on the floor.

Dunder Mifflin's Chief Financial Officer, David Wallace, is hosting a manager's cocktail party at his home in Mount Vernon. Jan and Michael decide to go to the party as a couple, ready to make their relationship public. As No. 2 in Scranton, Jim has to go, and he is unthrilled with the idea of discussing paper in his leisure time with people he doesn't know and doesn't care about. Michael invites and carpools with Dwight and they arrive so early that the hostess answers the door in her bathrobe. Michael offers his store-bought potato salad with the caveat that its' been in his car all day.

Pam and Roy have an argument with results in him promising to "do boyfriend things".

At the party, Dwight asks the host some fairly inappropriate and tactless questions about his home. Michael paws Jan, who then reverse-psychologies him by acting inappropriately until he becomes uncomfortable.

Meanwhile, the rest of "The Office" is enjoying themselves at Poor Richard's Pub. Creed runs into some underage patrons who bought fake Ids from him, and Toby tries to win a stuffed animal for Pam.

Back at the party, Karen runs into several former flames, describing all of them in detail to Jim, and then tells him that she had been playing a joke on him the whole time. He doesn't seem to find it very funny.

Back at Poor Richard's, Pam tells Roy she wants to do what it takes to make sure their relationship will work. In the interest of getting everything out in the open, she tells Roy what went down with her and Jim on Casino Night. Roy throws is beer bottle at the mirror and Pam breaks up with him. He destroys the bar in a fit of rage and his brother pays off the bar for damages. Roy realizes that all of their Jet-ski money is completely gone but consoles himself with the knowledge that he is going to kill Jim.

Trivia

J. J. Abrams, the director of this episode, is the creator of "Lost".

Michael toasts Lee Iacocca and "his failed experiment" the De Lorean, but Iacocca had nothing to do with the De Lorean.

This is the first episode to feature Poor Richard's Pub, an actual pub in Scranton.

The drinking game played at the bar is called "Up Jenkins!"

Pam's drawing now appears in "The Office".

David Wallace's son is played by Owen Daniels, the son of show creator Greg Daniels

The Negotiation

This is the eighteenth episode of the third season of "The Office". It was written by Michael Schur and directed by Jeffrey Blitz.

Synopsis

Roy attacks Jim for kissing Pam but Dwight saves him from Roy by spraying Roy with pepper spray. Jim feels guilty for all the tricks he has played on Dwight and apologizes. This attack leads to Roy's dismissal, and his duties are given to Darryl.

Darryl asks for 10% raise but is rejected. He realizes that corporate won't give him the raise he wants because it would make him higher-paid than Michael, and his solution is to pressure Michael into demanding his own raise. Michael, Toby and Darryl drive to Corporate Headquarters to negotiate Michael's raise. Michael's negotiation skills are woefully inadequate but Jan ends up giving Michael a 12% raise—the maximum he is entitled to.

In the break room, Pam apologizes to Jim but Jim seems cool and distant. Soon after, Roy asks Pam if they can meet for coffee. She confirms that it's over, and that she wants Jim. In "The Office", Jim sees Dwight and Angela kissing. He decides that he will never torment Dwight about this relationship, nor tell anyone about it, and this means that he is no longer in Dwight's debt.

The next day Andy returns from anger management, and, on his way in, Dwight sprays him with pepper spray. Toby then confiscates a stun gun, a boomerang, handcuffs, a nightstick, a pair of brass knuckles, numchucks, throwing stars, and a samurai sword from Dwight's weapons cache.

Trivia

Ryan's middle name is Bailey.

Safety Training

This is the nineteenth episode of the third season of "The Office". It was written by BJ Novak and directed by Harold Ramis.

Synopsis

Andy returns from anger management counseling just in time for Safety Day, and requests that "The Office" call him Drew. Dwight decides to shun Andy for three years and refuses to call him Drew. Michael takes the staff of the upper office into the warehouse so they can learn about warehouse safety. Darryl reiterates over and over again that Michael is not allowed to touch, operate, or use the heavy machinery, and Michael keeps interrupting until Lonny loses his temper and insults him. In a talking head interview, Darryl tells us that he is on crutches because Michael pulled a ladder out from under him as a joke.

Next, "The Office" staff is treated to safety tips from Toby. Bored, they begin betting on a variety of topics to fill the betting vacuum that has arisen since the conclusion of March Madness. Jim, Kevin, Karen and Oscar bet on how many jelly beans are in Pam's candy dish. Kevin loses to Jim and says it's because he spends a lot of time at Pam's and has had ample opportunity to stare at the candies. Karen is not happy to hear this. Other bets include guessing how long Kelly can talk about Netflix, how many times she says awesome, and how many romantic comedies she discusses. The final bet is whether Creed will notice if someone switches his apple with a potato. He does not. Karen loses every bet.

Michael, feeling slighted that Darryl has characterized the upper office as far safer than the warehouse, concludes that depression is a safety hazard that the upper office workers endure more often than the warehouse workers. He plans to demonstrate the dangers of depression by jumping off the roof and landing on a trampoline. However, when he and Dwight test the trampoline with a watermelon, the watermelon bounces off and on Stanley's car, so they replace the trampoline with a bouncy house without testing it. Darryl, worried that Michael will hurt himself by jumping, talks Michael out of his fake "suicide attempt", by convincing him that he is braver than Darryl.

Deleted Scenes

Andy tries to remain calm when Kevin takes the last of the coffee.

Extension of Michael and Dwight in the hallway discussing how they should respond to Darryl's accusations.

In a talking head interview, Michael shows how safety training can be funny by talking like Borat—referencing Not Jokes in particular.

Several members of "The Office" staff take turns trying to talk Michael down from the roof.

Memorable Quotes

Andy Bernard: Several weeks ago, Andy Bernard had an incident. But after five weeks in anger management, I'm back. And I've got a new attitude, and a new name. And a bunch of new techniques for dealing with the grumpies.

Andy Bernard: You can call me Drew.
Jim Halpert: No, I'm not gonna call you that.
Andy Bernard: Cool. I can't control what you do, I can only control what I do.
Jim Halpert: Andy.
Andy Bernard: Drew.

Dwight Schrute: I was shunned from the age of four until my sixth birthday for not saving the excess oil from a can of tuna.

Dwight Schrute: Jim, could you please inform Andy Bernard that he is being shunned?
Jim Halpert: Andy, Dwight says welcome back and he could use a hug.
Dwight Schrute: Okay, tell him that that's not true.

Michael Scott: You don't go to the science museum and get handed a pamphlet on electricity. You go to the science museum, and you put your hand on a metal ball, and your hair sticks up straight...and you know science.

Michael Scott: I think that everybody is going to vomit due to boredom.

Michael Scott: Heart disease kills more people than bailers.
Lonny: That's called having a fat butt, Michael.
Michael Scott: No, no, it's...
Lonny: Yeah, yeah. That's fat butt disease. That's what you suffering from? Fat butt disease, Michael?

Dwight Schrute: When you land, try and land like an eight-year-old. These bouncy castles aren't made for adults.

Dwight Schrute: Want to do another test? I've got plenty of watermelons in my trunk.

Dwight Schrute: I'm temporarily lifting the shun.
Andy Bernard: Thank you.
Dwight Schrute: Means nothing. I need you to do something for me.
Andy Bernard: Anything.
Dwight Schrute: Okay, calm down. I need you to acquire an inflatable house and/or castle.
Andy Bernard: You mean a moon bounce.
Dwight Schrute: What do you think? You've got an hour.
Andy Bernard: I'm gonna need petty cash.
Dwight Schrute: Shunning resumed.

Andy Bernard: Do you want a drawbridge?
Dwight Schrute: Un-shun. Yeah, that sounds good. Re-shun.

Dwight Schrute: Hey guys, listen up. Michael is up on the roof and acting strange.

Andy Bernard: Whoa, what's the situation?
Dwight Schrute: Un-shun. I think he's suffering from depression. Re-shun.

Andy Bernard: Okay, when's this shunning thing going to end?
Dwight Schrute: Un-shun. Never. Re-shun.

Dwight Schrute: Depressed? Isn't that just a fancy word for "bummed out"?
Michael Scott: Dwight, you ignorant slut!

Jim Halpert: I thought that the first run was a little dry, but they really hit stride with this one. I'm thinking about bringing my parents to see the matinee tomorrow.

Michael Scott: I "Braveheart." I am.

Michael Scott: I saved a life -- my own. Am I a hero? I really cant say...but, yes.

Product Recall

This is the twentieth episode of the third season of "The Office". It was written by Justin Spitzer and Brent Forrester, and directed by Randall Einhorn.

Synopsis

Jim starts out his day dressing as, and mimicking Dwight. Soon, however, Dunder Mifflin has to put out a serious fire when it is discovered that some paper has been released with an obscene watermark: a cartoon duck and a cartoon mouse in flagrante delecto.

Michael talks to the press while Jim and Andy soothe a school principal who used the paper for prom invites. While at the high school, Andy notices that his "girlfriend" is a student there, and his day goes downhill from there.

Meanwhile, Kelly has to teach Oscar, Kevin, and Angela, to handle the unending flow of customer support calls that are coming in due to the obscene cartoon debacle. Angela doesn't seem terribly serious in her apologies to customers for the company's mistake, Oscar seems to handle the calls well, and Kevin simply repeats his apology over and over again with no variation.

A customer comes to "The Office" to accept an apology in person and get a novelty check to repay her for the obscene paper she had purchased. Under the watchful gaze of a single reporter from the Scranton Times, Michael apologizes but she refuses his apology and calls for his resignation. Dwight tries to talk her out of this by reminding her that the cartoon sex appears consensual. Michael then makes a video in which he reiterates the fact that the mistake was not his fault and that he has become an "escape goat."

Meanwhile, Creed, who as Quality Assurance failed to catch the error, gets a farewell card for the complaining customer and money from all the employees to pay her off and go away. On his way out, Creed pockets the money and tosses the card.

Later, in the car, Jim cajoles Andy into singing "The Lion Sleeps Tonight" to cheer him up. And in the closing, Dwight comes to work dressed as Jim and imitates him.

Trivia

Towards the end, when Michael is reading off the cue cards, the second cue card says:

"I need this job. My mortgage is hundreds of dollars a month. With this job I can barely cover that. I have a company car, but I still have to pay for the gas. Gas prices are high and I have no savings whatsoever. And it wasn't even me. It is so not fair that they want me to resign."

Memorable Quotes

Jim Halpert: [dressed as Dwight Schrute] Question: What kind of bear is best?
Dwight Schrute: That's a ridiculous question.
Jim Halpert: False. Black bear.
Dwight Schrute: That's debatable. There are basically two schools of thought...
Jim Halpert: Fact: Bears eat beets. Bears. Beets. "Battlestar Galactica".
Dwight Schrute: Bears do not...what is going on? What are you doing? Well, imitation is the sincerest form of flattery, so I thank you.
(Jim pulls a bobblehead on his desk)
Dwight Schrute: Identity theft is not a joke, Jim! Thousands of families suffer every year!
Jim Halpert: Michael!
Dwight Schrute: Oh, that's funny. Michael!

Michael Scott: We have a crisis. Apparently a disgruntled employee at the paper mill decided that it would be funny to put an obscene watermark on our 24-pound cream letter stock. 500 boxes have gone out with the image of a beloved cartoon duck performing unspeakable acts upon a certain cartoon mouse that a lot of people like. I've never been a fan.

Creed: Every week, I'm supposed to take four hours and do a quality spot-check at the paper mill. And of course the one year I blow it off, this happens.

Andy Bernard: William Doolittle at your service. AKA Will Do.
Jim Halpert: Yeah, I'm definitely going to go alone.
Michael Scott: No, no, I need two men on this. That's what she said. No time! But she did. No time!

Creed: The only difference between me and a homeless man is this job. I will do whatever it takes to survive...like I did when I was a homeless man.

Kelly: Look, I know the reason that you guys became accountants is 'cause you're not good at interacting with people. But guess what? From now on, you guys are no longer losers. So gives yourselves a round of applause.
Oscar: I wonder how many phone calls you're missing while you're teaching us to answer calls.
Kelly: I know, right? Probably a lot.

Dwight Schrute: I grew up on a farm. I have seen animals having sex in every position imaginable. Goat on chicken. Chicken on goat. Couple of chickens doing a goat, couple of pigs watching. Whoever did this watermark got it exactly right.

Michael Scott: Mrs. Allen is our most important client. Because every client is our most important client. Even though she's a pretty unimportant client really

Andy Bernard: One of your students is a bitch.

Jim Halpert: Andy is having a real rough day today.

Andy Bernard: I want to take out an ad in your yearbook. Full page, two words.

Jim Halpert: Good luck.

Andy Bernard: That's not what I had in mind.

Women's Appreciation

This is the 21st episode of the third season of "The Office". It was written by Gene Stupnitsky and Lee Eisenberg and directed by Tucker Gates.

Synopsis

Phyllis is flashed in "The Office" parking lot and Michael wonders why anyone would want to flash Phyllis. He then puts his finger through his fly and pretends that the flasher is back. After realizing that these gaffes could be construed as sexual harassment and get him fired, Michael fakes feminist indignation and then orders everyone into an impromptu seminar on the everyday prejudices that women face. As the self appointed speaker at said seminar he then makes some more sexist comments and then offers to take the women to the place that they, as women, would feel the most comfortable: the mall. Although they consider the offer extremely condescending, the mall sounds better than "The Office" and they agree to go.

Dwight orders Pam to make a sketch of "the pervert" and she draws a picture of Dwight -- but, with a mustache and without glasses. Dwight and Andy put of the fliers locally and then Andy says he would like to take some of the fliers and post them near where he lives (close to a school).

Michael, meanwhile, receives aggressive booty calls from Jan, which her Hunter had put on her schedule. Over lunch at the food court, Michael shares some intimate details about him and Jan and the women encourage him to weigh the pros and cons of his relationship. He does so and slowly reveals that Jan is sexually controlling in ways that humiliate him. Karen tries to give Michael reasons to stay and work things out with Jan. Pam urges that his relationship with Jan is unhealthy. Finally, Michael flatly says that he's not happy around Jan, and the women convince him that this "con" outweighs all of the "pros."

To thank them for their advice, Michael ,oblivious to the inappropriateness of the gesture, treats the women to one item each at Victoria's Secret. Karen buys some sexy lingerie for her and Jim's six-month anniversary and Pam buys a fuzzy bathrobe that she will cut into towels.

At "The Office", Kevin, Jim, Ryan and Toby hang out in the women's room, Creed enters, and is forced to tell the group that he uses the women's room to "go number 2". Ryan admits to Jim that he'd asked Karen out via email once. Jim awkwardly replies that Karen had already read it to him, and that "she liked him as a friend."

On the way back from the mall, Meredith's minivan breaks down, and Michael is unable to change the tire. Pam changes it herself. Upon returning to "The Office", Michael decides to call Jan and end their relationship as he begins to leave the break-up message on his voicemail, Jan enters "The Office". She tells Michael that she feels badly about their earlier conversation regarding the booty call, so she drove all the way from New York City to apologize. Michael accepts her apology and just as he does so, her cell phone alerts her to a voice mail from Michael. When she hears the message she hangs up the phone; looking hurt, she leaves Michael's office silently.

The episode ends with Jim telling Dwight that he saw the pervert above the sink in the women's bathroom. Dwight storms into the bathroom, where a mustache has been drawn with marker on one of the mirrors. When he sees his reflection line up with the mustache, Dwight realizes he was duped by Pam and it was his face that appeared on the flyers.

Trivia

Dwight Schrute's cell phone number can be briefly glimpsed on a flier warning about the parking lot pervert. Calling the number (1-800-984-3672) connects to a voicemail message, with special information about his pervert task force, a message reaching out to the pervert, and an offer to sell his 1985 maroon Firebird and/or Dunder Mifflin paper products.

Memorable Quotes

Dwight Schrute: I wish I could menstruate. If I could menstruate, I wouldn't have to deal with idiotic calendars anymore. I'd just be able to count down from my previous cycle. Plus I'd be more in tune with the moon and the tides.

Michael Scott: My point is...a penis when seen in the right context is the most wonderful sight for a women. But when seen in the wrong context it's like a monster movie.

Pam: Can you tell us what happened?
Phyllis: Umm, I was walking to the building and this man asked me for directions. And he was holding a map. And when I walked over, he had it out... on the map.
Angela: Phyllis, you're a married woman.
Creed: The guy was just hanging brain. I mean, what's all the fuss?
Creed: If that's flashing, then lock me up.

Michael Scott: Women can't have fun if they don't feel safe. For example, Jan and I have a safe word in case things go too far. Foliage. And if one of us says that word, the other one has to stop. Although last time, she pretended she didn't hear me.

Dwight Schrute: You know what? Why doesn't Oscar run the meeting? He's a homosexual.
Jim Halpert: Why don't you run the meeting? You play with dolls.

Dwight Schrute: Those are collectible action figures. And they're worth more than your car.

Michael Scott: You know what? I am the expert. I will conduct it. I know the crap out of women

Michael Scott: What is a Pap smear? Or is it "schmear?" Like cream cheese.

Michael Scott: Cons. Wears too much makeup. Breasts - not anything to write home about. Insecure about body. I'm unhappy when I'm with her. Flat-chested.

Pam: What was the last one?

Michael Scott: She's totally flat. Shrunken chesticles.

Beach Games

This is the 22nd episode of the third season of "The Office". It was written by Jennifer Celotta and Greg Daniels and directed by Harold Ramis.

Synopsis

As has become the norm, Michael claims to feel sick shortly after being given some paperwork. Soon, Dunder Mifflin CFO David Wallace calls and Michael uses this opportunity to brag about dumping Jan. David tells Michael that he's invited to interview in a week's time for a promotion at corporate headquarters in New York City.

This means that Michael will have to select someone to manage "The Office" in his absence. To pick the pro-tem manager, Michael has decided to conduct a Survivor-like game at Scranton Lake. The winner will get to be the manager. Michael wants everyone to think of the outing as a day off -- except for Pam who is to take notes on each participant/contestant.

As they arrive at the lake Michael selects four employees "at random" to lead different "tribes": Jim, Dwight, Andy and Stanley. Michael explains their pros and cons to the camera: Jim has a great personality but doesn't work hard because he can finish a project in thirty minutes and that same project would take Michael all day; Dwight is enthusiastic but "an idiot"; Andy "gets" Michael, but he doesn't trust Andy; and Stanley represents the 'amazing progress of African-Americans'. The tribes they form are named "Gryffindor", led by Dwight, "Voldemort", led by Jim, "Blue Team", led by Stanley, and "Team U.S.A.", led by Andy.

In an egg race, Jim tricks Karen—who is blindfolded-- into stepping into the nearby lake; Andy can't stop Kelly from removing her blindfold; and Stanley sits out since he doesn't feel like doing anything. Michael then decides to have a hot dog eating contest but the employees give it a thumbs-down and refuse to participate. Irritated, Michael tells the group of his interview and explains that the winner of the games would replace him. The teams then become more enthusiastic.

Privately, Dwight directs Angela, who is on Andy's team, to pretend to not hear, or hear incorrectly, everything that Andy says. Michael busts out novelty sumo wrestling suits for the sumo competition. Dwight wins and Andy falls in the lake and begins drifting away. Karen and Jim sneak away to phone headquarters, making appointments for the same open interview that Michael was invited to.

The final challenge is a walk across hot coals. Pam wants to try but Michael stops her since she is not one of the candidates. Jim refuses but, Dwight decides to go for it. The heat surprises him and he collapses on the hot coals.

Michael than announces the next event—a sudden death standup comedy competition, and then Jim and Karen reveal that they will also be in New York City for the open interviews at corporate. Pam, still at the coals, decides to run across. This emboldens her and she rebukes the staff for not attending her art show and reveals that she called off her wedding because of Jim. She goes on to claim that it's "fine" that he's with someone else now, and then decides she needs to walk in the water to cool her feet. Michael is impressed but reiterates that he is looking for a replacement with sales experience.

Trivia

"The Flintstones" sing-along at the end of the show recalls a scene in the movie "Planes, Trains & Automobiles" where John Candy's character leads a bus full of strangers in singing the song.

Memorable Quotes

Michael Scott: To what do I owe this great honor, David Wallace?
David Wallace: Michael, I am calling...
Michael Scott: And Gromit.

Michael Scott: Oscar, you brought your Speedo, I assume?
Oscar: I don't wear a Speedo, Michael.

Michael Scott: Well, you can't swim in leather pants. Ha ha! I'm just yanking your chain. Not literally.

Michael Scott: Today, we are not just spending a day at the beach.
Stanley: Oh sweet mother of God.
Michael Scott: If you don't like it, Stanley, you can go to the back of the bus.
Stanley: Excuse me?
Michael Scott: Or the front of the bus. Or drive the bus.

Pam: Hey, I want to say something. I've been trying to be more honest lately and I just need to say a few things. I did the coal walk! Just, I did it. Michael, you couldn't even do that. Maybe I should be your boss. Wow, I feel really good right now. Why didn't any of you come to my art show? I invited all of you. That really sucked. It's like sometimes, some of you act like I don't even exist. Jim, I called off my wedding because of you. And now we're not even friends. And things are just like weird between us, and that sucks. And I miss you. You were my best friend before you went to Stamford. And I really miss you. I shouldn't have been with Roy, and there were a lot of reasons to call off my wedding. But the truth is, I didn't care about any of those reasons until I met you. And now you're with someone else and that's fine. It's... whatever. That's not what I'm... I'm not... okay, my feet really hurt. The thing that I'm just trying to say to you, Jim, and to everyone else in the circle, I guess, is that I miss having fun with you. Just you, not everyone in the circle. Okay, I am gonna go walk in the water now. Yeah, it's a good day.

Michael Scott: Pam, that was amazing. But I am still looking for someone with a sales background.

The Job

This is the 23rd and final episode of the third season of "The Office". It was written by Paul Lieberstein and Michael Schur and directed by Ken Kwapis.

Synopsis

Michael arrives at corporate headquarters for his promotion interview – but only realizes once he is there that he is one day early, and has to turn around and go back to Scranton.

Feeling confident that he got the job, Michael sells his condo on eBay for 80% of what he paid and names Dwight as his successor.

Jim walks in with a polished new 'do, saying that Karen advised him that his old 'do said "homeless" and he wants something that says "successful." Still dealing with the aftermath of her true confession at the beach, Pam apologizes to Karen, explaining that she is not sorry about what she said, only that she had put Karen in such an awkward position. In an interview, Karen calls Pam "kind of a bitch."

In an attempt to get Michael to take her back, Jan arrives at "The Office" fresh from a few days off. Pam tells Michael to be strong and to not get back together with her. At first, he listens to her but then caves after he realizes that Jan had her boobs done.

Soon after, Jim and Karen leave to spend the night in New York City. She tells Jim that if either of them gets the job, both should move to New York but Jim doesn't seem too happy about that prospect.

Back in Scranton, Dwight names Andy as his number 2 and gives Pam the role of "Secret Assistant to the Regional Manager."

Dwight then begins to devise more compulsory meetings, and passes out Shrutebucks for good behavior. Ultimately deciding that the stick is a better motivator than the carrot, he and Andy repaint the walls of the regional manager's office black in order to instill fear.

During his interview at Corporate, Michael learns he is interviewing for Jan's job; she is to be fired. Michael immediately goes and tells Jan, who interrupts Karen's interview. Jan refuses to leave, and is escorted out by security.

Michael learns he won't get the job, and as he and Jan drive to Scranton, Jan ponders making their relationship her "full-time job" He drops her off and returns to the Scranton office and says he will be there forever and tells Ryan to get him some coffee.

Karen completes her interview and takes off to have lunch with friends while Jim is interviewing. Jim's interview with David begins very well. When asked for his sales report numbers, Jim sees that Pam had written an encouraging note, along with enclosing a yogurt lid medal from Office Olympics. Jim stumbles throught the rest of the interview. When it ends, Jim drives straight back to Scranton, appearing to have forgotten about Karen, and asks Pam to dinner.

The episode ends with CFO Wallace offering the job over the phone to Ryan, who accepts and breaks up with Kelly within minutes.

Trivia

The fake web address Ryan invented for Creed's blog is "www.creedthoughts.gov.www/creedthoughts". NBC created the Creed Thoughts blog when the episode aired. Its initial entry is identical to the one the character was in the middle of writing during the episode.

Memorable Quotes

Michael Scott: I have got it made in the shade. I know this company. The other branch managers are total morons. Hey Pam, yeah. I forgot what day the interview was and I drove to New York accidentally. Be like three hours late.

Pam: Umm, about the beach...
Karen: It's okay. We all say things without thinking.
Pam: Oh no, it's not that. I've actually been thinking that for a long time and I'm glad I said it. I just... I'm sorry if it made you feel weird.

Karen: Oh, okay.

Karen: Pam is... kind of a bitch.

Ryan Howard: Last year, Creed asked me how to set up a blog. Wanting to protect the world from being exposed to Creed's brain, I opened up a Word document on his computer and put an address at the top. I've read some of it. Even for the Intranet, it's...pretty shocking.

Dwight Schrute: Welcome to the Hotel Hell. Check in time now. Check out time is never.
Jim Halpert: Does my room have cable?
Dwight Schrute: No, and the sheets are made of fire!
Jim Halpert: Can I change rooms?
Dwight Schrute: No, we're all booked up. Hell convention in town!
Jim Halpert: Can I have a late check out?
Dwight Schrute: I'll have to talk to the manager.
Jim Halpert: You're not the manager...even in your own fantasy?
Dwight Schrute: I'm the owner....co-owner. With Satan!
Jim Halpert: Okay, just so I understand it... in your wildest fantasy, you are in hell. And you are co-running a bed and breakfast with the devil.
Dwight Schrute: But I haven't told you my salary.
Jim Halpert: Go
Dwight Schrute: Eighty thousand dollars a year!

Dwight Schrute: Once I'm officially Regional Manager, my first order of business will be to demote Jim Halpert. So I will need a new number two. My ideal choice? Jack Bauer. But he is unavailable. Fictional. And overqualified.

Andy Bernard: I am a great interviewee. Why? Because I have something no one else has - my brain. Which I use to my advantage when advantageous.

Dwight Schrute: When you have done something good, you will receive one Schrute buck. One thousand Schrute bucks equals an extra five minutes for lunch.

Index

Andy, 5, 6, 11, 29, 32, 35,
47, 55, 57, 58, 62, 65,
68, 69, 74, 77, 82, 83,
84, 86, 88, 89, 90, 91,
93, 95, 96, 97, 98, 99,
102, 103, 104, 106,
111, 113, 116, 123,
124, 125, 126, 128,
130, 131, 133, 134,
135, 136, 138, 139,
140, 141, 146, 167,
168, 169, 170, 171,
172, 173, 174, 175,
177, 178, 179, 186,
191, 195
Angela, 5, 7, 10, 16, 17,
18, 20, 22, 25, 27, 28,
30, 31, 33, 40, 53, 55,
61, 63, 64, 67, 68, 72,
92, 93, 95, 98, 101,
102, 103, 104, 105,
107, 108, 110, 118,
123, 124, 126, 127,
128, 129, 130, 134,
135, 138, 145, 146,
148, 159, 161, 167,
174, 182, 186
Angelina Jolie, 16, 84
Ben Franklin, 142, 143,
144, 145, 146, 149
Bob Vance of Vance
Refrigeration, 7, 14, 46,
155

Carol, 18, 28, 44, 56, 57,
58, 60, 63, 64, 65, 66,
67, 68, 100, 105
CIA, 101, 106
coffee, 34, 71, 76, 80, 81,
85, 124, 126, 128, 129,
130, 167, 169, 192
Cornell University, 11
corporate, 100, 101, 105,
123, 126, 127, 135,
166, 185, 187, 190
Creed, 7, 13, 17, 25, 31,
35, 39, 40, 41, 51, 63,
76, 77, 78, 86, 92, 94,
108, 109, 137, 139,
153, 160, 164, 169,
175, 177, 180, 182,
183, 192, 193
Darryl, 103, 116, 119,
120, 166, 168, 169, 170
David, 163, 165, 185, 188,
192
Dunder-Mifflin, 36, 37, 38,
45, 47, 49, 51, 73, 74,
77, 89, 92, 96, 100,
101, 118, 120, 125, 126
Dwight, 4, 6, 7, 8, 9, 11,
13, 14, 16, 17, 18, 19,
20, 21, 23, 25, 26, 28,
29, 30, 32, 33, 34, 35,
36, 37, 38, 39, 40, 41,
42, 44, 45, 46, 47, 48,
49, 50, 51, 52, 53, 56,

59, 61, 71, 72, 73, 75,
76, 78, 79, 80, 81, 82,
83, 84, 85, 86, 88, 90,
91, 93, 95, 98, 100,
101, 102, 104, 106,
107, 108, 109, 111,
112, 113, 115, 116,
120, 121, 123, 124,
125, 127, 128, 129,
130, 131, 132, 133,
134, 135, 136, 137,
138, 139, 140, 141,
143, 144, 145, 146,
148, 149, 150, 151,
152, 153, 154, 155,
157, 159, 161, 162,
163, 164, 166, 167,
168, 169, 170, 171,
172, 173, 174, 175,
176, 177, 178, 179,
181, 182, 183, 186,
187, 190, 191, 194, 195
Entourage, 27, 31, 32
Hannah, 86, 87, 92, 95,
102, 103, 113
Jamaica, 105, 114, 117
Jan, 6, 8, 18, 20, 24, 27,
28, 30, 33, 34, 36, 44,
48, 71, 72, 74, 75, 76,
79, 80, 86, 92, 114,
115, 119, 120, 121,
122, 125, 127, 130,
145, 163, 164, 166,
180, 181, 183, 185,
191, 192
Jell-O, 6, 45

Jerome, 18, 22, 26
Jim, 4, 5, 6, 7, 8, 9, 10,
11, 12, 13, 14, 17, 18,
19, 20, 21, 23, 24, 25,
29, 31, 32, 33, 35, 36,
39, 44, 45, 47, 48, 49,
52, 53, 55, 57, 58, 61,
62, 64, 65, 68, 69, 71,
73, 74, 75, 77, 80, 82,
83, 84, 85, 86, 87, 91,
93, 94, 95, 96, 97, 98,
99, 101, 102, 103, 104,
105, 106, 107, 108,
109, 110, 111, 112,
113, 114, 115, 119,
123, 124, 125, 126,
128, 129, 130, 132,
133, 134, 135, 136,
137, 138, 140, 141,
142, 143, 144, 145,
147, 148, 149, 150,
151, 154, 157, 159,
161, 163, 164, 166,
167, 168, 170, 171,
173, 174, 175, 176,
177, 178, 180, 181,
183, 185, 186, 187,
189, 190, 191, 192,
194, 195
Josh, 18, 19, 23, 29, 35,
55, 61, 74, 80, 83, 92,
96, 98, 138
Karen, 5, 31, 32, 35, 36,
39, 45, 47, 55, 57, 58,
59, 62, 68, 69, 71, 74,
82, 85, 86, 87, 91, 92,

94, 101, 102, 103, 104,
105, 110, 111, 113,
114, 116, 124, 126,
128, 129, 130, 134,
136, 142, 143, 144,
158, 159, 160, 164,
168, 180, 186, 187,
190, 191, 192, 193
Kelly, 6, 17, 20, 29, 34,
51, 53, 55, 56, 57, 58,
59, 60, 61, 62, 63, 65,
66, 67, 72, 73, 77, 84,
85, 93, 97, 107, 126,
138, 152, 154, 156,
159, 161, 169, 174,
177, 178, 186, 192
Kevin, 5, 20, 23, 24, 27,
30, 37, 39, 49, 55, 61,
63, 64, 78, 83, 88, 89,
92, 94, 95, 99, 102,
103, 104, 108, 115,
122, 123, 134, 140,
144, 152, 168, 169,
174, 180
Martin, 5, 17, 25, 36, 40,
86, 87, 90, 93, 94, 95,
96, 99
Meredith, 17, 25, 29, 59,
63, 76, 84, 98, 103,
110, 139, 148, 152,
159, 161, 181
merger, 83
Michael, 4, 6, 7, 8, 10, 11,
12, 13, 14, 15, 16, 17,
18, 19, 21, 22, 23, 24,
25, 26, 27, 28, 30, 32,

34, 35, 36, 37, 38, 39,
40, 41, 42, 43, 44, 45,
46, 47, 48, 49, 51, 52,
54, 55, 56, 57, 58, 59,
60, 61, 62, 63, 64, 65,
66, 67, 68, 69, 71, 72,
73, 74, 75, 76, 77, 78,
79, 80, 82, 83, 84, 85,
86, 87, 88, 90, 91, 92,
93, 94, 95, 96, 97, 98,
99, 100, 101, 102, 103,
104, 105, 106, 107,
109, 110, 112, 113,
114, 115, 116, 117,
118, 119, 120, 121,
122, 123, 124, 125,
127, 128, 130, 131,
133, 134, 135, 136,
137, 138, 139, 140,
141, 142, 143, 144,
145, 146, 147, 148,
149, 150, 151, 152,
153, 154, 155, 156,
157, 158, 159, 160,
161, 162, 163, 164,
165, 166, 168, 169,
170, 171, 173, 174,
175, 176, 177, 178,
179, 180, 181, 182,
183, 185, 186, 187,
188, 189, 190, 191,
192, 193
Mr. Brown, 8, 12
Oprah, 16
Oscar, 4, 6, 7, 8, 9, 10, 11,
12, 89, 105, 108, 133,

134, 136, 137, 138,
139, 140, 146, 160,
168, 174, 178, 183, 188
Pam, 4, 5, 6, 7, 8, 9, 10,
12, 16, 17, 19, 20, 21,
22, 23, 26, 27, 29, 31,
34, 37, 38, 42, 44, 45,
46, 48, 49, 52, 56, 57,
59, 60, 61, 65, 67, 68,
69, 73, 75, 78, 82, 83,
85, 87, 92, 93, 94, 95,
96, 100, 101, 102, 103,
104, 105, 106, 109,
110, 111, 114, 115,
116, 117, 118, 120,
121, 123, 124, 126,
128, 129, 130, 135,
136, 138, 139, 142,
143, 144, 145, 147,
149, 152, 153, 154,
156, 157, 160, 163,
164, 165, 166, 167,
168, 179, 180, 181,
182, 183, 185, 187,
189, 190, 191, 192, 193
Phyllis, 7, 14, 20, 26, 29,
34, 39, 46, 64, 86, 102,
103, 108, 109, 113,
124, 126, 129, 135,
139, 142, 143, 151,
152, 153, 154, 155,
160, 179, 182
Robert Mifflin, 47, 51, 53
Roy, 5, 6, 21, 29, 37, 56,
73, 78, 105, 115, 119,
144, 153, 154, 157,
160, 164, 166, 167, 189
Ryan, 4, 7, 8, 11, 13, 16,
17, 19, 20, 34, 37, 44,
45, 46, 47, 48, 49, 50,
51, 52, 53, 56, 59, 65,
67, 72, 73, 77, 86, 94,
95, 97, 99, 102, 103,
107, 110, 112, 113,
124, 125, 130, 131,
133, 134, 143, 144,
145, 146, 154, 157,
158, 159, 162, 167,
180, 192, 193
Sandals, 101, 105, 117
Scranton, 5, 18, 19, 20,
24, 28, 29, 30, 34, 35,
38, 51, 71, 72, 73, 74,
75, 77, 78, 79, 80, 82,
83, 85, 86, 87, 100,
106, 116, 126, 140,
163, 165, 175, 185,
190, 191, 192
Stamford, 4, 5, 6, 8, 9, 11,
12, 18, 19, 23, 29, 35,
36, 45, 47, 55, 57, 62,
71, 72, 74, 75, 79, 82,
83, 86, 87, 90, 92, 110,
116, 129, 137, 189
Stanley, 6, 14, 20, 26, 37,
46, 49, 53, 54, 60, 71,
72, 75, 80, 81, 86, 92,
94, 96, 102, 109, 110,
113, 117, 124, 125,
160, 169, 186, 188

Staples, 19, 74, 83, 89,
    133, 136, 139, 140
The Daily Show, 88
Toby, 4, 6, 12, 15, 19, 20,
    23, 24, 37, 55, 63, 72,
    76, 82, 84, 90, 95, 98,
    100, 101, 105, 108,
    114, 146, 152, 154,
    164, 166, 167, 168, 180
Todd, 143, 147, 148
waitresses, 104, 106

www.ingramcontent.com/pod-product-compliance
Lightning Source LLC
Chambersburg PA
CBHW031146160426
43193CB00008B/273